Deconstructing Power and Isms within the Church and Society

Christine A. Smith

Deconstructing Power and Isms within the Church and Society

Judson Press has made every effort to trace the ownership of all quotes. In the event of a question arising from the use of a quote, we regret any error made and will be pleased to make the necessary correction in future printings and editions of this book.

Interior design by Crystal Devine.
Cover design by Danny Ellison.

Library of Congress Cataloging-in-Publication data

Names: Smith, Christine A., author.
Title: Deconstructing power and isms within the church and society / Christine A Smith.
Description: Valley Forge, PA : Judson Press, [2025] | Includes bibliographical references.
Identifiers: LCCN 2024051421 (print) | LCCN 2024051422 (ebook) | ISBN 9780817018535 (trade paperback) | ISBN 9780817082604 (epub)
Subjects: LCSH: Intercultural communication--Religious aspects--Christianity. | Social justice--United States. | Marginality, Social--United States. | Power (Social sciences)--United States. | Ideology--United States.
Classification: LCC BR115.C8 S5825 2025 (print) | LCC BR115.C8 (ebook) | DDC 261.8/38--dc23/eng/20250128
LC record available at https://lccn.loc.gov/2024051421
LC ebook record available at https://lccn.loc.gov/2024051422

Printed in the USA.

First printing, 2025.

I dedicate this book to my parents,
Patricia Helena Garraway Small and
Robert Alexander Small,
who both taught me to love God,
treat people with compassion and respect,
and be grateful that I was born an American citizen
in the greatest country in the world.

Contents

Introduction

I have given them your word and the world has hated them, for they are not of the world any more than I am of the world. My prayer is not that you take them out of the world but that you protect them from the evil one. They are not of the world, even as I am not of it. Sanctify them by the truth; your word is truth. As you sent me into the world, I have sent them into the world. For them I sanctify myself, that they too may be truly sanctified. —John 17:14-19

As Jesus prayed to the Father in preparation for his earthly departure, he shared these words. Jesus expressed that he had given his disciples his Father's words and that the world hated the disciples because they were not of the world. Across the generations, Christians have struggled with this notion of being in the world but not *of* the world. Jesus' words were as radical then as they are now. He challenged the religious leaders of the day for their mistreatment of marginalized people and the neglect of the poor. He healed people on the sabbath, allowed children to come to his teaching sessions, ate with tax collectors, and dined with people of ill repute. He even allowed a questionable woman to wipe his feet with her hair! He told a parable in which a Samaritan was the story's hero. Jesus was radical. He threatened the established order of the religious leaders and the Roman Government. In short, Jesus was messing up their political system and their money pipelines!

Jesus was *in the world*, but Jesus was not governed by the corrupt world systems of greed, oppression, injustice, and inequality. In this work, *Deconstructing Power and Isms within the Church and Society*, we explore further Jesus' call to God's people to stand up against sacred and secular systems of false piety and oppression. What exactly is false piety? At times, false piety appears as fake religion, wolves in sheep's clothing, and people using God's Word or the church to advance selfish, evil ambitions. At other times, false piety manifests in misguided people who perceive their attitudes and behaviors to be in line with patriotism and or godliness. They are unaware that they have been largely influenced by racist, sexist, and xenophobic ideas that drive their hatred and ignorance. False piety will be discussed further in Chapter 1.

In 2013, Judson Press published my first book, *Beyond the Stained Glass Ceiling: Equipping and Encouraging Female Pastors.*[1] I wrote this book to address the struggles that women who felt led to serve as senior pastors experienced. Moving past the obvious barriers of bad theology and patriarchal systems, the book explored underlying issues that are not readily apparent, significantly impacting opportunities for women to be called to stable, healthy, strong congregations. Over one hundred women from various racial backgrounds and ethnicities were surveyed. Despite their cultural, ethnic, and racial differences, one factor remained consistent: glass ceilings limited or altogether barricaded doors of opportunity for their advancement.

Beyond the Stained Glass Ceiling featured words of wisdom, caution, encouragement, and specific steps or recommendations for women to take advantage of the opportunities that did exist. The book encouraged women to work together and to resist patriarchal and racist teachings that often pit women and marginalized groups against one another. Those who are in the position of being power brokers were encouraged to come alongside women pastors, not only with verbal support but with practical, tangible actions to open doors to greater opportunities.

In my first book, I also invited male senior pastors who have been actively involved in leveling the playing field for women pastors to share their strategies and recommendations for their male colleagues in ministry, congregations, and search committees. We celebrated the strides that have been made by women pastors up to that point, the success stories of women being called to more stable, healthy congregations, and the heights that have been reached by women, on a number of fronts. Naturally, we acknowledged that we still have many more rivers to cross.

Through *Deconstructing Power and Isms within the Church and Society*, I seek to expand the conversation beyond the plight of women pastors, to delve more deeply into exploring structures that perpetuate the oppression of women, Brown and Black people, and the poor, through false piety. In ecclesiastical realms, some feign godliness by donning the appearance of being holy while they tie proverbial millstones around the necks of the marginalized and disinherited. In secular realms, others find themselves committing insurrections in the name of God and patriotism. Others push so-called peace and harmony through subterfuge and cosmetic diversity. Taken together, system perpetrators maintain power by stoking divisions that oppress specific groups of people in the name of righteousness.

Throughout scripture, God encourages, admonishes, compels, and commands the people of faith to look out for, create opportunities for, and when necessary, provide for those who are hungry, destitute, imprisoned, impoverished, and sidelined. Through the prophets, God expresses anger toward those who practice false piety. God warns them to take away their songs and hymns of praise sung while neglecting the needs of those who are marginalized and oppressed. Jesus himself calls the Pharisees whitewashed sepulchers because they practiced a false religion. He calls them snakes because they exploited the people with their excessive demands and regulations while doing nothing to care for their physical or spiritual needs.

Today, false piety manifests in a variety of ways. Recent occurrences point to those who continue to deny systemic racism, sexism, and oppression in America while feigning godly principles. A decade after *Beyond the Stained Glass Ceiling* was published, women have indeed made great strides. In 2020, Attorney Kamala Harris became the first Black and Southeast Asian woman to be elected Vice President of the United States of America. Women have increased in the House of Representatives and the Senate. Currently, twelve women—all white—serve as governors. In the ecclesiastical realm, more economically stable, healthy, and flourishing congregations are calling women into pastoral leadership roles. Some denominations are calling women to serve as executive ministers and presidents of fellowships and ecclesiastical bodies. We give God praise for each of these milestones.

However, even after discussing the great accomplishments that women have made, we would be derelict in our duty if we did not acknowledge the intense struggles that women, Black and Brown people, and the poor (often one in the same) continue to face, and the ground that we have lost. A major denomination, the Southern Baptist Convention (SBC) recently expelled churches that had the audacity to hire or call women to serve in any pastoral positions. The US Supreme Court overturned *Roe v. Wade*, stripping away the decades-long rights of women to have control over their reproductive health. Politicians and other public figures demonize and mischaracterize Planned Parenthood as simply being an abortion, baby-killing establishment, after providing necessary, critical, low-to-no-cost healthcare and educational services to underserved women and communities over many decades. Extremists target physicians, the lives of workers are threatened, their clinics are set on fire, and their funding is drastically reduced—all in the name of godliness.

Our nation is currently backpedaling on the rights of women as well as other marginalized groups. The US Supreme Court also gutted Affirmative Action, making it illegal for colleges and universities to consider race in their admissions process. Books are being banned and described as woke or anti-American if they present the historical realities of systemic racism, white privilege, sexism, xenophobia, or anything dealing with the LGBTQ+ community—all in the name of false piety.

America is rapidly becoming an authoritarian state, overly influenced by fake holiness and white nationalism. Legislative measures that would provide for affordable healthcare, a clean environment, common-sense gun control, and equitable educational systems for our children are lobbied against by many of the same individuals aligned with the religious right, who proudly describe themselves as pro-life, as they vote for life-defying measures.

Lest we become daunted by words shrouded in gloom and doom, there is some GOOD NEWS! We *do* have a say in the matter. If we recognize the storm is already here and the massive tsunami approaching, we can prepare ourselves and engage in intentional discussions, prayerful, well-thought-out strategies, and plans to dismantle systems that perpetuate injustice and inequality. In this book, we offer examples of the aforementioned struggles that we continue to face. We also highlight factors that contribute to our current situation, discussing practical measures that can be taken to thwart their progress. Finally, we offer strategies and recommendations for specific actions that individuals and groups can take within their particular contexts to influence change. At the end of each chapter, we offer questions and discussion starters for groups.

I am indebted to those community leaders, both in the ecclesiastical and secular realms, who have partnered with me to provide words of insight, instruction, and encouragement to help us make a difference in this season and beyond. In this next chapter, we will take a deep dive into the ways that pseudo-godliness and powerful systems link forces to oppress many.

NOTE

1. Christine A. Smith, *Beyond the Stained Glass Ceiling: Equipping and Encouraging Female Pastors* (Judson Press, 2013).

Section One

False Piety and Power: How They Work

CHAPTER 1

Why We Need This Discussion Now

These people honor me with their lips,
but their hearts are far from me.
They worship me in vain;
their teachings are merely human rules. —*Matthew 15:8-9*

We are now experiencing the coming to the surface of a triple-prong sickness that has been lurking within our body politic from its very beginning. That is the sickness of racism, excessive materialism, and militarism.

—Martin Luther King Jr.[1]

A False Piety Story

Approximately twenty-two years ago, I was hired to work in a women's shelter as a pastoral counselor. The shelter was affiliated with a local mission. The shelter focused not only on providing temporary housing and basic needs but also a Christian witness. In addition to what they called the day program, where women could stay up to one week (they had to leave during the day and return by certain hours in the evening), the shelter offered a long-term program that lasted approximately eighteen months.

The long-term program offered free housing, meals, and educational training programs. Nursery and preschool services were provided for women with small children. The program helped mothers with older school-age children register their children at nearby schools. As a part of the program requirements, all women participated in chapel services and Bible studies. The facilities were clean, fresh, and aesthetically beautiful. On the surface, it seemed like a wonderful place to work. The program leaders appeared genuinely concerned about helping the women rise out of poverty while gaining the love, support, and compassion of Christian people.

I was excited and honored to be hired to work in such an amazing program—until I learned what was happening behind closed doors. As I participated in the interviews where women applied to the program, I watched as women were told one thing, only to have something altogether different happen. The program promised women that they would receive training appropriate to their educational levels. Some women had experience with Microsoft programs (Word, Excel, PowerPoint, etc.). They had already taken classes at local colleges or universities. They were excited to learn that they would be given an opportunity to take additional classes toward a certificate or an associate degree.

However, once they entered the program, they were denied the promised opportunities to continue to pursue their education. Instead, they were forced to take classes offered through the mission program, using software developed by their mission's network. Women with college-level training were forced to take classes with illiterate women. Several residents came to me in tears, showing me the work where they were being taught how to spell *cat* and *dog*. Several of us working as pastoral counselors spoke with the administration about these concerns. We were told the women needed to work their way up through the program. They refused to allow them to move up, despite their abilities.

The facility had a state-of-the-art computer lab. The company that donated the computers offered to load the Microsoft Suite software on each computer. Initially, the program leaders refused. After several meetings and requests to give women more opportunities to learn the program and to have volunteers come in to teach them, we had a breakthrough. Several of the women took advantage of the classes. We also included classes on résumé writing and interview best practices. We partnered with a local chapter of Dress for Success to provide women with the appropriate clothing for interviews.

To celebrate the accomplishments of the women who completed the series, we arranged for a "pamper me" day. We identified professionals who would volunteer their time to come in and give the women facials, hand and neck massages, and foot soaks. We planned for a luncheon, complete with certificates and a guest speaker to lift and encourage the women to go higher. We were all excited! But then, we were called into a special meeting with the mission's CEO. He informed us that he did not agree with our celebration plans. I shall never forget his reasoning. He said, "Why would you expose these women to facials and massages? You are just going to cause them to be frustrated because they will not be able to have those things when they leave the program." WHAT? We were appalled! He had low expectations for these women, and therefore, he wanted to keep a ceiling above their heads that blocked them from seeing themselves in arenas far beyond a homeless shelter and mission program.

The mission leaders' idea of success was simply becoming a Christian, learning some scripture passages, and getting off drugs. Perhaps many of these leaders could not conceive of the program participants going higher because many mission workers were uneducated. Many came from the streets, joined some evangelical church, were given a new dress, suit, and tie, and placed in positions of authority. THAT was *their* idea of success. Sadly, many both in the church and in the world become nervous if they see people rising higher than their status, abilities, or boundaries imposed upon them by themselves or others. The mission program leaders believed themselves righteous, holy, and dutiful. They were blind to their oppressive, sexist, and unjust treatment of the program participants.

In some instances, women program leaders treated the participant women harshly. For example, a young woman who had given birth just before being accepted into the program became extremely ill and had to be hospitalized. Upon returning to the shelter, she was still weak and sickly. It was evident that she needed rest and at least a week to recuperate. The counselors arranged for around-the-clock support for her and her newborn. In a surprise move, the program administrator reprimanded us for doing so. She canceled the schedule we prepared for individuals to volunteer to help.

When I asked about the decision, the administrator said that if the woman were home sick with a newborn, she would have to take care of the baby by herself. She said the young woman needed to learn the skills necessary to care for her child even when she is weak and sick. While that may sound admirable, it was in fact cruel. The young woman could barely hold her head up. She was weak from vomiting and dehydration (as a side note here, often, the poor and people of color do not receive the care they need in hospitals and are released much too soon). She could have dropped the baby or passed some illness to her child. We ignored the foolish administrator's decision and sneaked around to give the woman the support she needed.

Although there are many, the last example I will share is one of the most devastating. During an interview with a young mother, she explained that two of her children had breathing conditions that required aerosol treatments. I was familiar with this process because one of my children had a similar issue. She explained that the children needed to have their treatments before they ate, which may require her to come to lunch a little late. She also shared that her children had food allergies, and she would purchase their special diet items with her food stamps. Everyone agreed this would be permissible, and the woman and her children were admitted into the program.

The woman attended classes and complied with the requirements of the schedule. However, as she explained in the interview, she was about fifteen minutes late to lunch each day, as she needed to give her children their breathing treatments. Lunch aides began to complain that her "tardiness to lunch" was hindering their ability to clean up the lunchroom. In truth, they wanted the residents to hurry up and finish so they could leave early.

Even more troubling was that some other mothers complained that their children were jealous because this woman's children received different kinds of food to eat. Therefore, the administrator decided that her children could no longer eat their special food. They would only be allowed to drink the milk, juice, water, and food provided by the mission. The young mother became frantic. She came to me afraid, angry, and tearful. She had nowhere else to go, and her children were allergic to the food prepared at the facilities. I made a decision that may not have been advisable, but nonetheless, I made it. I spoke with the daycare provider in the basement and asked if she would place the young woman's special meals in their refrigerator and allow her to come and get her children's food from there.

A maintenance woman saw me meeting with the daycare director and us bringing the food to the refrigerator. She went to her supervisor and told what she saw. Program leadership called me into a meeting, where they reprimanded me and gave me my walking papers. They kicked the young woman out of the program. I was stunned and disillusioned, along with this young woman, for a season. This act was done by people who misunderstood Christ's love in action. They were convinced that my acts of holy defiance were arrogant and wicked. These three personal experiences at the mission are examples of false piety and highlight important aspects of disenfranchisement, neglect, and abuse in the name of Christianity.

False Piety, Patriotism, and Oppression in American Churches and Society

Piety—faithfulness to something to which one is bound by pledge or duty.[2]

The actual term "piety" only appears once in the Bible: 1 Timothy 5:4, from the King James Version:

> But if any widow have children or nephews, let them learn first to shew piety at home, and to requite their parents: for that is good and acceptable before God.

Here, the term is consistent with the Latin pietà, which means pity or compassion and a sense of duty, religiousness, loyalty, and patriotism. The *Pietà* is also the name of the late-fourteenth century marble sculpture by Michelangelo of Mary holding the dead body of her son, Jesus.[3]

The term "pious" has roots in both French and Latin. From the French, being pious was associated with mercy, tenderness, and pity. In the late 1500s, piety in English was associated with dutiful behavior toward family members, country, and God.[4]

Many in the sacred and secular realms have taken the concept of piety—duty, loyalty, mercy, compassion, and patriotism—and sullied its intended usage. Just as ancient religious and corrupt political leaders during biblical times took what was meant for good and, in turn, used it for evil, many in the twenty-first century are doing the same. Their acts are in no way examples of piety but rather cruelty. We can surmise then that *false piety* extracts any notion of mercy, tenderness, and compassion, and replaces those descriptors with a twisted sense of patriotism, a perverted sense of loyalty and duty, and an oppressive, distorted picture of a god that does not reflect the *agape* love of the true God.

Why We Need This Discussion Now

Martin Luther King Jr. delivered one of his most revolutionary speeches in 1967 during the National Conference on Politics held in Chicago, Illinois. He challenged his audience to consider what he called, "the three evils of society: racism, excessive materialism, and militarism."[5] If we are honest, we must admit that the social construct of race, and the proliferation of oppressive, white male-dominated systems, coupled with the rise of false piety, continue to tyrannize America. When we elected Barack Obama as our first Black president in 2008, many believed that we had finally overcome racism. And while it was indeed an extraordinary feat, Obama's election revealed an infestation that had simply been waiting to emerge—the racist divisions continue to run deep.

Poverty levels have risen exponentially, and another civil war in the US appears to be looming. Due to the Trickle Down Economics policies of the late former President Ronald Reagan, the gains made by a great number of Americans through the New Deal, the policies of the late former President Franklin Delano Roosevelt, have all but been decimated. According to the Economic Policy Institute, CEOs were paid 399 times more than the average worker in 2021. That number represents a 1,460 percent increase since 1978.[6] Certainly, this is a manifestation of King's prophetic words regarding excessive materialism and greed. Any reference to these disproportionalities is characterized as unpatriotic by the ignorant or those who benefit from economic injustice. Sadly, some in the church have turned a blind eye to these evils and coddled those peddling racism and various forms of oppression.

Racism intersects with gender and class to create formidable systemic barriers that perpetually keep us divided. Identity politics has constructed high walls, thick ceilings, and glass cliffs for many. The glass cliff is the notion that women more often than men are appointed to lead unstable, dysfunctional organizations.[7] Both ecclesiastical and secular realms have misinterpreted biblical texts to justify slavery, the oppression of women, and poverty-inducing/perpetuating systems in the US. It is important to explore the concept of piety. The rise of false piety coupled with white nationalism following the Obama presidency has shaped our society for the foreseeable future. Unbridled hate speech, otherisms, and right-wing politics against women, Black and Brown people, and the poor are essential elements of that reshaping.

These evils exist in both the church and the world. We must take time now to reflect upon the historical context of the issues and factors that have brought us to where we are today. If we do so, we may just have a chance to dismantle the threatening systems that will chokehold future generations.

Biden Out, Harris In, and the Reelection of Trump

As the 2024 presidential election cycle began, many questioned whether then-President Joe Biden was the best messenger and leader for the Democratic Party. In 2020, Biden presented himself as a one-term president who would serve as a bridge for the next generation. But somewhere along the line, that narrative changed, and he decided to run again.

The presidency ages all persons sitting behind the Resolute Desk. This fact became increasingly clear as an already-aged President Joe Biden defiantly declared his intentions to run for a second term in office. At eighty-one, President Biden would have been the oldest candidate to ever run for president. If he were to win, he would have been eighty-six at the close of his second four-year term. In addition to his chronological age, Biden was becoming increasingly visibly frail. News clips of him tripping over his feet or falling up the Air Force One stairs or of him calling Vice President Harris, "Vice President Trump," during a news conference fueled concerns that the White House was deliberately hiding his declining mental acuity.

Rumors swirled that Biden needed to be replaced at the top of the presidential ticket. Many continued to stand behind and with the president, until they did not. The fateful day that sealed his eventual exit from the race was imminent. The first of its kind presidential debate featuring an incumbent president and a former president was high-stakes media. Many were concerned that Trump would not control himself and harm his presidential bid. Others held their breath, whispering prayers that Biden would not lose his train of thought and make embarrassing bumbles.

Unfortunately for Biden, the latter came to pass. All played well for Donald Trump. Biden was unable to clearly and coherently complete his sentences. He ended his statements well before the time on the clock allotted for him to speak. Although Trump provided little substance in his responses and spewed ridiculous lies throughout the debate, the focus was placed on Joe Biden. The White House countered that President Biden was exhausted from his travel schedule and still recovering from a cold. Those reasons did not fly with the public.

Long story short, over thirty Democratic House members, a few Senators, and notable figures in Hollywood (George Clooney, for example) began insisting that President Biden step aside. High-profile donors threatened to dry up donations as long as he remained atop the ticket. Additionally, some started suggesting that within four weeks, the Democrats needed to have mini primaries or scheduled debates to replace Biden. There was only one problem with this unrealistic agenda. The person next in line was Vice President Kamala Harris. Pundits believed that the country would never vote for a Black woman. Old and ugly rumors (fueled by Trump and some of his followers) that Harris slept her way to the top splashed across social media platforms and some news outlets. Trump even tried to reinflict the birtherism argument upon voters, arguing Harris was not born in the United States. Harris, the daughter of a Southeast Asian mother and a Jamaican father, was born in Oakland, California. He used the same argument against former President Barack Obama, who was born in Hawaii.

Trump also asserted he did not know if Harris was Indian or Black. He claimed, during the National Association of Black Journalists conference, that she formerly called herself Indian, but now she calls herself Black. Both Harris and her sister affirmed that their mother raised them as Black women. Harris has notably embraced her racial identity as Black. She attended an HBCU (Historically Black College or University), pledged and became an AKA (one of the Black Greek Divine Nine sororities), and regularly self-identified as a Black woman. Trump must have forgotten the one-drop rule (the Southern rule, upheld in the courts, that a single drop of Black blood made a person Black).[8] Apparently, now this rule only applies when it is convenient.

Billionaire Elon Musk resorted to using artificial intelligence (AI) on his social media platform to create pictures depicting Harris wearing a baseball cap with a hammer and a sickle on the front, suggesting that she was a communist. The post was viewed over 60 million times, according to Musk's platform X (formerly known as Twitter). Further, using misogynistic language, Musk, the so-called richest man in the world and Trump endorser, reportedly stated that women should not take part in democracy.[9]

Questions about Harris's preparedness, strength, and ability to be viewed as a world leader abounded. Trump's running mate, J.D. Vance, argued that nobody would want to join the military under a President Harris. Vance claimed that she was not concerned about the military but was more concerned about gender issues and making the armed services more inclusive. Vance argued further that America would not be safe under her leadership. It did not matter that Harris was an attorney, a prosecutor, a district attorney, the attorney general of one of the top three largest states in the country, California, a US senator, and the Vice President of the United

States. Vice President Harris, with all of that, somehow, was *still* not prepared or qualified in their eyes.

Ultimately, President Biden, in his own way and on his own terms, made the painful decision to step aside. But he did something that would change the course of history: he endorsed Vice President Kamala Harris. With Biden's endorsement, a growing drumbeat of thousands rallying around her, young voters, Black women, "White Chicks," "Black Men," and "White Dudes" for Kamala, scattered and ill-advised plans to find someone else were brought to a screeching halt. Within a couple of weeks, Harris wrapped up the nomination and made history once more. She became the first Black and Southeast Asian woman to become the nominee of a major political party.

Interestingly, I heard a woman news commentator muse out loud, "As brilliant and prepared as Vice President Harris is, she is still grossly underestimated. I wonder how many other Black women have this experience?" I found her line of thinking utterly unbelievable. I thought to myself, "Dear white sister, you have no idea!" Though genuine, her question was emblematic of the larger problem—so little appears to be known about how Black women feel, in their own words.

Harris's rallies were electric. Hope and excitement filled the air. Hollywood high-powered actors and business moguls got on board. It felt like we were on our way to electing the country's first Black and Southeast Asian woman. But it was not to be. On Tuesday, November 5, 2024, to the shock, disappointment, and anguish of many, America reelected former President Donald J. Trump—something thousands of Americans hoped would never happen again. To explore how this reelection became a reality, we must consider the backdrop of his first presidency. We also need to understand how racism, sexism, otherisms, and false piety converged to douse any real hope that a woman—a Black and Southeast Asian woman—would become the next American president in 2025.

The Aftermath of the Obama Presidency

How did we get here? Many believe it started with a backlash against the Obama presidency. In 2016, many Americans believed that we were on the verge of electing our first woman president in the history of the country. Former First Lady, US Senator, and Secretary of State Hillary Rodham Clinton became the first female nominee of a major political party when the Democratic National Convention nominated her. Arguably, Secretary Clinton was one of the most qualified individuals to ever run for the presidency. On the other side, business tycoon, millionaire, CEO, and host of the television series *The Apprentice*, Donald Trump, was (to the chagrin of many Republicans) the Republican nominee.

Donald Trump was known for his vulgar and brutish behavior. He had the reputation of being a womanizer. He had three wives with three sets of children. His business dealings were questionable. Many in the Black community reviled him for being a racist because he paid thousands of dollars for full-page ads in New York newspapers calling for the reinstatement of the death penalty after five African American and Latino young men known as the "Central Park Five" were accused of brutally raping a white woman jogger in Central Park.[10] Although there were no eyewitnesses, inconsistent stories, and no DNA evidence, the young men were arrested and wrongfully imprisoned, some for over a decade.[11] When the actual perpetrator of the crime came forward and admitted his guilt, exonerating the young men from the crime, Trump refused to apologize and recant his devastating statements and inflammatory rhetoric.

At the time, political polls all agreed that there was no way that *this* man could ever be elected as the President of the United States of America. Secretary Clinton had a commanding lead in most reputable polls. However, on November 8, 2016, many Americans received the shock of their lives. Although Secretary Clinton won the popular vote, Donald

Trump acquired the necessary Electoral College votes (270, and he won 304) to become the forty-fifth US president. He had no prior record of public or military service. Publicly, so many stood against him. People from his own political party warned that electing such a person would signal the downfall of our democracy. What we did not know was that *privately*, many white Americans and Evangelical Christians were galvanizing a political revolution the likes of which we had not seen since before the Civil Rights Movement.

The Trump Factor

A significant segment of the white population became nervous after the election of the forty-fourth president, Barack Obama. Many believed the false narrative initiated and advanced by Donald Trump that President Obama was not a US citizen. He openly and forcibly demanded that President Obama show his long-form birth certificate, proving his birthplace was in America (Obama was born in Hawaii). Trump also peddled lies that Obama was a Muslim, participating in the Islamic religion (Obama is a practicing Christian). He emphasized Obama's middle name, Hussein, regularly as he spoke, stirring up fear, hatred, and Islamophobia among many.

Memorably, during the 2008 presidential campaign, Obama's opponent was the late Senator John McCain. Among his party and beyond, McCain was a well-respected war hero, described as a maverick because of his willingness to break from the Republican party to stand upon his principles. He was the epitome of "country before party." In a notable instance, which some would say cost him the US presidency, McCain refused to go along with a woman at one of his rallies when she said that she could not trust then-Senator Obama because he was an "Arab." Another man said that he and others were scared of someone (Obama) who "consorts with terrorists." McCain famously responded by saying that Obama is a "decent family man, a citizen who just happens to have different political views." He encouraged his followers to be respectful and not to embrace racial phobias.[12] In another instance, McCain stood with the Democrats and voted for the Affordable Care Act. His vote helped to ensure that the bill would be passed into law.

Then-citizen Trump used fear as a powerful mobilizer and motivator. Political scientist Charles Tien, along with professor of criminal justice Alexander H. Updegrove and his co-authors, argue that racial resentment has increased toward minorities since the election of former President Barack Obama. They assert that President Obama's election unleashed years of anxiety and fears among white Americans that minorities would overrun the country and displace them.[13] Further, they believe that white women, fearing lost opportunities for their men as minorities advanced, were drawn to Trump's white supremacy rhetoric.[14]

Truths of Tien and Updegrove's arguments concerning white women embracing Trump's rhetoric were borne out in 2024. Statistics showed that, percentage-wise, white women supported Democratic candidate Kamala Harris's platform concerning bodily autonomy, which is a woman's right to choose what happens to her body, particularly as it relates to abortion. In seven out of ten states where abortion restrictions were on the ballot, initiatives supporting bodily autonomy passed instead.[15]

In five out of those seven states, however, while voting for women's rights, a large percentage of those women voted for Trump at the top of the ticket. While Harris made inroads with white suburban women and men, 53 percent of white women and 60 percent of white men voted for Trump. Slightly more than half of white women voted for Trump.[16]

One could reasonably draw a direct correlation between the prior election of Donald Trump and past presidency of Barack Obama. Although many white Americans voted for President Obama, a new reality seemingly set in once he actually *became* president of the country. Suddenly, the reality of a "browning population" became too close to home. The majority culture struggled to envision a time when white people would no longer dominate.

With the passage of the healthcare bill, known as the Affordable Care Act, some politicians persuaded people to believe they would lose control over their choices for healthcare providers. With the Supreme Court's decision to allow same-sex marriages, evangelical Christians feared that their children would be severely harmed and corrupted. With the passage of the Lilly Ledbetter Fair Pay Act,[17] CEOs of large corporations feared what they considered to be frivolous lawsuits and millions of dollars of lost revenue. White nationalists feared that their country was being taken from them and turned over to "the n-word."

Many white evangelical Christians completely overlooked Donald Trump's outrageous, sinful, illegal actions because of his promise to deliver a conservative US Supreme Court. For decades, they laid the groundwork for overturning *Roe v. Wade*—the law that gave women the right to an abortion. Many pro-life believers saw Donald Trump as a savior of sorts during a time when they were filled with fear and anxiety over losing their "Christian nation." Historians James L. Gorman, Jeff W. Childers, and Mark Hamilton found a strong correlation between the political leanings of Christians and the color of their skin.[18]

Donald Trump did not single-handedly create the quagmire of fears described above. His audacious, irreverent, and bullish voice emboldened and unleashed sentiments brewing for some time. There was a time when people may have *felt* a certain way about those different from themselves, but there was still an apprehension about declaring their beliefs boldly and publicly. During and since the first Trump presidency, tendencies toward racism, sexism, and otherisms have become full-throated, public attacks.

During Trump's first term in office, he fulfilled his promise to appoint additional conservative judges to the Supreme

Court and federal benches. With three new conservative justices, the pendulum of the highest court in the land swung hard right. Laws once perceived as settled became unraveled. Fearful of the Trump base (MAGA, the abbreviation for Make America Great Again), right-wing politicians abandoned any willingness for common-sense compromises between the two major political parties.

Interestingly, extreme right religious leaders and white nationalists hold in common their beliefs that their stances are righteous and admirable. Often, you will see a convergence of the cross and the flag as symbols of piety and patriotism. In July 2023, country music singer Jason Aldean's song "Try That in a Small Town" was pulled from the Country Music Awards because of the thinly veiled racist verbiage and imagery used. The song champions vigilantism, warning so-called criminals against car-jackings, burning flags, spitting on cops, and more in a "small town." The music video features riots, Black Lives Matter protests, and the singer performing in front of the Maury County Courthouse in Tennessee, known for the historical lynching of an eighteen-year-old Black man falsely accused of attacking a white girl.[19] Since the condemnation of the music video, the song topped the iTunes Top Songs and Videos chart, nabbing the number one spot in July 2023.

Numerous examples highlight the critical nature of this conversation now. Consider the following. In the name of righteousness, many pro-lifers denounce abortion in almost all situations. While some accept the exceptions of rape, incest, or the life of the mother, others do not. Some are calling for a complete federal ban on all abortions. If this were to happen, many Black, Brown, marginalized, and impoverished women would die. The wives, daughters, and sisters of hypocritical, wealthy politicians and even some Christians will secretly travel to private doctors or other parts of the world to get their procedures done. The less fortunate will be forced to resort to crude, self-inflicted wounds or back-alley facilities to get the help they need.

Oppression in the name of righteousness is not new. Corrupt religious leaders across the ages have taken sacred texts and manipulated them to benefit themselves and to assert power over others. Jesus reprimanded the Pharisees for their hypocrisy in honoring God with their words but dishonoring God with their actions. When the Pharisees questioned Jesus about not enforcing their religious traditions with his disciples, Jesus, in turn, questioned them concerning their nullification of God's laws with their human rules.

In Matthew 15, Jesus confronted the religious leaders' assertion that people could avoid caring for (honoring) their parents' financial needs if they say that the money they would have used to take care of them is "devoted to God." The implication is that the money could then go to the religious leaders with no concern for others. Here, we see corrupt leaders twisting God's word to benefit themselves. Therefore, Jesus quoted the Old Testament prophet Isaiah, condemning the people for honoring God with their lips but not with their hearts (Isaiah 29:13).

In like manner, today's culture has no shortage of false prophets and teachers, holding monetary prayer lines, promising a husband, a house, a car, a million-dollar windfall, etc., if desperate people "sow a seed" of $250, $500, $1,000, or purchase prayer cloths and holy oil to aid them in their impoverished conditions and distress. While the biblical concept of tithing is holy and honorable, established by God to support the priests, the work of the ministry (aiding the poor, the widows, the community), and the maintenance of God's house, the aforementioned tactics used by religious charlatans is abhorrent in the sight of God. Ezekiel 22:12-14 declares,

> In you are people who accept bribes to shed blood; you take interest and make a profit from the poor. You extort unjust gain from your neighbors. And you have forgotten me, declares the Sovereign Lord.

> I will surely strike my hands together at the unjust gain you have made and at the blood you have shed in your midst. Will your courage endure or your hands be strong in the day I deal with you? I the Lord have spoken, and I will do it.

In the same way, corrupt secular leaders have used symbols and sentiments of patriotism and loyalty to God and Country to pit groups of oppressed people against one another. Statistics reveal that large numbers of uneducated, poor, white people support Trump. Although he is a millionaire, Trump was able to convince this demographic that the elites would never look out for their needs. He convinced them that Brown people were taking over our country, bringing in drugs, raping women, committing crimes, and taking their jobs. Pew Research Center reports that the margin of whites without a college degree who voted for Trump was the largest since the 1980 exit polls.[20] The hope for a post-racial America following the Obama presidency crumbled fast.

President Trump was able to manipulate a specific group of white people—those afflicted with the legitimate pain and oppression felt by *all* impoverished people, but conditioned by deep-seated, well-watered racism, stereotypes, and the need to feel like they are better than somebody. He pounced upon their vulnerabilities, convincing them that they were true patriots who needed to help him defend our country, build the wall, and make America great again! Trump promoted a racial tribalism of sorts, an us versus them mentality, launching the MAGA movement.

Today's American society appears to have a confluence of duty and religion, heavily tilted toward patriotism in relation to piety. Kristin Kobes Du Mez, in *Jesus and John Wayne: How White Evangelicals Corrupted a Faith and Fractured a Nation,* relays that white men in the evangelical realm were disturbed by the images of a demure, seemingly weak Jesus depicted by historical artworks. Instead, they advanced imagery of a rugged, "militant masculinity, an ideology that enshrines patriarchal authority and condones the callous display of power, at home and abroad" over the years. Du Mez further suggests that "family values" conservatives were drawn to Trump because of his domineering demeanor, lack of concern for how others perceived him, and his promises to deliver on the right-wing political wish list. They exchanged the "Jesus of the Gospels" with a "vengeful warrior Christ."[21]

In both instances, false piety is at play, manifesting as wicked intentions masquerading as godly or righteous devotion. One need not dig too deeply beneath the surface of history to identify how false piety, both in the sacred and secular realms, has been used to advance oppression, marginalization, and disenfranchisement of specific groups of Americans. As we have read, false piety and systemic racism, along with other isms, work hand in hand to hoodwink groups of people to fight each other, rather than recognizing common enemies that stoke their fears and hatred toward one another.

On the other hand, former Georgia state representative Stacey Abrams took a completely different approach as she ran for the governorship of Georgia. Rather than pit people against one another, Abrams reached out to all people. Her strategy was to help people, no matter their race, ethnicity, religious beliefs, etc., see the economic and social injustices that are plaguing our nation and impacting the lives of American citizens.[22] She inspired people to look beyond skin color and see how people of all stripes were being economically depressed and disenfranchised, enduring voter suppression, stripped of their rights, and being broken by current systems. Because of her approach, Black, Brown, Asian, Jewish, and white people all came together to rally behind the issues and vote.[23]

Although Abrams did not become governor, her political machine helped Georgia turn from red to purple, altering the trajectory of Georgia politics, at least during that election cycle. Through her efforts, Georgia elected its first Black senator,

Raphael Warnock, and first Jewish senator, John Ossoff, in its history. Her admirable, powerful, and change-initiating work exemplifies how others can begin to upend systems of oppression and disenfranchisement. Her work embodies the words of Jesus when he declared, "The King will reply, 'Truly I tell you, whatever you did for one of the least of these brothers and sisters of mine, you did for me'" (Matthew 25:40).

MUCH work still needs to be done across America. In July 2023, the US Supreme Court used verbiage from the 1896 *Plessy v. Ferguson* case that used the US Constitution Amendment XIV, which provides equal protection under the law, to justify stripping away the rights of colleges and universities to consider race in the admissions process. The Court argued that our Constitution already prohibits discrimination because of the amendment. Indeed, that very amendment allowed former slaves to have the right to vote and to be elected in the United States House of Representatives and the Senate during the Reconstruction Era. But history reveals how short-lived those rights were. Soon, the Jim Crow Era demolished those fragile gains, turning the concept of equal protection under the law upon its head.

Politicians, governmental leaders, complicit universities, businesses, etc., are leading the charge in denying people their rights because of ideologies and words taken out of context—the very words meant to promote equity and equality for all. Conservative politicians in America have furthered this false concept of equal protection for all Americans by denouncing the importance and intrinsic value of diversity. They have even used the words of Dr. King, stating that "we should not be judged by the color of our skin, but the content of our character."[24]

In August 2023, the American Alliance for Equal Rights (founded by anti–affirmative action activist Edward Blum) filed a lawsuit against the Fearless Fund, a fund that was established in 2019 by three Black women to award $20,000 to African American women entrepreneurs for business startups. In a shameless move, the American Alliance argued in the lawsuit that the fund runs afoul of the Civil Rights Act of 1866, which prohibits racial discrimination in contracts.[25] For a business to receive the funding, at least 51 percent of the ownership must be comprised of Black women. The Fearless Fund was created to counteract the well-established fact that formidable barriers persist for women of color and Black women, in particular. According to *Forbes* magazine, Black women business owners make roughly six times less than women-owned businesses. Approximately 3 percent of Black women-run businesses have survived beyond five years. Additionally, Black women receive less than 0.35 percent of all venture capital funding.[26]

In the face of these factors, right-leaning politicians and unscrupulous, greed-consumed organizations are pulling up all the stops to drag our nation back down into a whole that robbed women and people of color of their freedoms, legalized systemic racism, and used religion to justify ignorance and hate. Given all these blatant injustices, the Church and the broader society must do more than just pray and sing Kumbaya. Christians must embrace God's consistent word found throughout scripture, but most succinctly in Micah 6:8:

> He has shown you, O mortal, what is good.
> And what does the Lord require of you?
> To act justly and to love mercy
> and to walk humbly with your God.

For those who do not ascribe to Christian teachings but still embrace some genuine form of a moral compass, the mandate is to embrace mercy, compassion, and humanness. The preamble to the Declaration of Independence declares,

> We hold these truths to be self-evident, that all men are created equal, that they are endowed by their Creator

> with certain unalienable Rights, that among these are Life, Liberty, and the pursuit of Happiness.[27]

Both the biblical text and the moral mandate of equality in America's founding documents affirm the need for all citizens to stand, advocate, work, and agitate those who perpetuate systems of oppression, inequality, and injustice in our nation.

Questions and Discussion Starters

As we reflect upon historical and current events, we must ask ourselves some critical questions: How did we get here? In such a short period of time, how have we allowed our nation to lose so much ground in terms of civil rights? What strategies should we learn and use to help turn the tide? Below are questions to help you to contemplate, process, and share your thoughts.

1. In your view, how has false piety, coupled with power, contributed to the oppression of specific groups of people?
2. Have any of your personal, business, or community relationships been impacted by current-day politics? If so, how?
3. How would you describe "veiled oppression"? Discuss ways to "pull back the veil."
4. How can individuals and local groups promote diversity, equity, and inclusion in their contexts (i.e., in jobs, in schools, in religious groups)?
5. If America remains on the current track (in terms of false piety, power, and systems of oppression), what is your greatest fear for the next generation? List practical steps that individuals and groups can take to change the trajectory.

NOTES

1. History.com Editors, "Quotes from 7 of Martin Luther King Jr's Notable Speeches," *History*, 2022, https://www.history.com/news/martin-luther-king-jr-speeches.

2. "Piety," in *Merriam-Webster Dictionary*, 2022, https://www.merriam-webster.com/dictionary/piety#:~:text=a,%3A%20dutifulness%20in%20religion%20%3A%20devoutness.

3. Beth Harris and Steven Zucker, *Michelangelo, Pietà, marble, 1498-1500* (Saint Peter's Basilica, Rome), https://www.khanacademy.org/humanities/renaissance-reformation/high-ren-florence-rome/michelangelo/v/michelangelo-piet-1498-1500#:~:text=The%20Piet%C3%A0%20was%20a%20popular,she%20holds%20on%20her%20lap.

4. "Piety," *Online Etymology Dictionary*, 2022, https://www.etymonline.com/word/piety.

5. History.com Editors, "Quotes from 7 of Martin Luther King Jr's Notable Speeches," *History*, 2022, https://www.history.com/news/martin-luther-king-jr-speeches.

6. Josh Bivens and Jori Kandra, "CEO Pay has skyrocketed 1,460% since 1978," *Economic Policy Institute*, October 4, 2022, https://www.epi.org/publication/ceo-pay-in-2021/.

7. Thekla Morgenroth, Teri A. Kirby, Michelle K. Ryan, and Antonia Sudkämper. "The Who, When, and Why of the Glass Cliff Phenomenon: A Meta-Analysis of Appointments to Precarious Leadership Positions," *Psychological Bulletin* 146, no. 9 (2020), https://doi.org/10.1037/bul0000234.

8. F. James Davis, "Who Is Black? One Nation's Definition: The One Drop Rule defined," *PBS Frontline*, 1991, https://www.pbs.org/wgbh/pages/frontline/shows/jefferson/mixed/onedrop.html.

9. Donnie O'Sullivan, "Elon Musk's Attacks on Kamala Harris Become More Unhinged, with Help from AI," *CNN*, September 3, 2024, https://www.cnn.com/2024/09/03/media/elon-musk-x-kamala-harris-trump-misinformation/index.html.

10. Olivia B. Waxman, "President Trump Played a Key Role in the Central Park Five Case. Here's the Real History Behind When They See Us," *Time.com*, May 31, 2019, https://time.com/5597843/central-park-five-trump-history/.

11. History.com Editors, "Central Park Five: Crime, Coverage & Settlement | HISTORY." *History*. May 14, 2019, https://www.history.com/articles/central-park-five.

12. Matt Spetalnick, "Republican Anger Bubbles Up at McCain Rally," *Reuters*, October 13, 2008, https://www.reuters.com/article/business/media-telecom/republican-anger-bubbles-up-at-mccain-rally-idUSN10414512/.

13. Charles C. Tien, "The Racial Gap in Voting Among Women: White Women, Racial Resentment, and Support for Trump," *New Political Science* 39, No. 4 (2017): 651–69, https://doi.org/10.1080/07393148.2017.1378296.

14. Alexander. H. Updegrove, Maisha N. Cooper, Erin A. Orrick, and Alex. R. Piquero. "Red States and Black Lives: Applying the Racial Threat Hypothesis to the Black Lives Matter Movement." *Justice Quarterly* 37, No. 1 (2020): 85–108, https://doi.org/10.1080/07418825.2018.1516797.

15. Isabel Guarmieri and Krystal Leaphart, "Abortion Rights Ballot Measures Win in 7 out of 10 US States," *Guttmacher Institute*, November 2024, paragraph 1, https://www.guttmacher.org/2024/11/abortion-rights-state-ballot-measures-2024.

16. Center for American Women and Politics, "Gender Differences in 2024 Vote Choice Are Similar to Most Recent Presidential Elections," Rutgers-New Brunswick Eagleton Institute of Politics, December 28, 2024, para. 8, https://cawp.rutgers.edu/blog/gender-differences-2024-presidential-vote.

17. Daniel Kurt, "Lilly Ledbetter Fair Pay Act: Definition, History, Impact," *Investopedia,* October 15, 2024, https://www.investopedia.com/terms/l/lilly-ledbetter-fair-pay-act.asp#:~:text=our%20editorial%20policies-,What%20Is%20the%20Lilly%20Ledbetter%20Fair%20Pay%20Act%3F,under%20federal%20anti%2Ddiscrimination%20laws.

18. James L. Gorman, Jeff W. Childers, and Mark Hamilton, *Slavery's Long Shadow: Race and Reconciliation in American Christianity* (William B. Eerdmans Publishing Co.: 2019), 78–79.

19. Rebecca Carballo, "The History of the Lynching Site where Jason Aldean Filmed a Music Video," *New York Times,* July 21, 2023, https://www.nytimes.com/2023/07/21/arts/music/jason-aldean-song-video-lynching-courthouse-choate.html#:~:text=Henry%20Choate%2C%20an%2018%2Dyear,of%20attacking%20a%20white%20girl.

20. Alec Tyson and Shiva Maniam, "Behind Trump's victory: Divisions by Race, Gender, Education," *Pew Research Center,* November 9, 2016, https://www.pewresearch.org/short-reads/2016/11/09/behind-trumps-victory-divisions-by-race-gender-education/.

21. Kristin Kobes DuMez, *Jesus and John Wayne: How White Evangelicals Corrupted a Faith and Fractured a Nation* (Liveright, 2020), 2–3.

22. Donna Wong, "Asian Americans, Ya'll Turn Georgia Blue—Vote Stacey Abrams for Governor!" *Eastwind Politics & Culture of Asian America*, September 25, 2018, https://eastwindezine.com/asian-americans-yall-turn-georgia-blue-vote-stacey-abrams-for-governor/.

23. Molly Ball, "Stacey Abrams Could Become America's First Black Female Governor—If She Can Turn Georgia Blue," *Time,* July 26, 2018, https://time.com/5349541/stacey-abrams-georgia/.

24. For example, see Caitlyn Meisner, 2022. "Greg Abbott Rounds up McLennan County to Vote Conservative," *The Baylor Lariat.* November 3, 2022, https://baylorlariat.com/2022/11/03/abbott-rounds-up-mclennan-county-to-vote-conservative/.

25. The Associated Press, "Fund sued over grant program for Black women enlists prominent civil rights attorneys," *NBC News*, August 11, 2023, https://www.nbcnews.com/news/nbcblk/

fund-sued-grant-program-black-women-enlists-prominent-civil-rights-att-rcna99450.

26. Forbes EQ, “Investing in the future: How supporting Black women-owned businesses and entrepreneurs benefits us all,” *Forbes*, April 17, 2023, https://www.forbes.com/sites/forbeseq/2023/04/27/investing-in-the-future-how-supporting-black-women-owned-businesses-and-entrepreneurs-benefits-us-all/?sh=3355a9274ac2.

27. National Archives, “America’s founding documents: The Declaration of Independence,” *National Archives,* https://www.archives.gov/founding-docs/declaration.

CHAPTER 2

Bad Theology and Power Structures

"Certain seeds it will not nurture, certain fruit it will not bear and when the land kills of its own volition, we acquiesce and say the victim had no right to live."

—TONI MORRISON, *THE BLUEST EYE*[1]

In the world, but not of the world . . .
A holy identity

They are no more defined by the world
Than I am defined by the world.
Make them holy—consecrated—with the truth;
Your word is consecrating truth.
In the same way that you gave me a mission in the world,
I give them a mission in the world.
I'm consecrating myself for their sakes
So they'll be truth-consecrated in their mission.

—John 17:16-19, MSG

During one of the Progressive National Baptist Convention's "Compelling Preaching Series" events at Olivet Institutional Baptist Church, in Cleveland, Ohio, Otis Moss Jr. (Pastor Emeritus, OIBC) was the main lecturer. The topic was "Prophetic Preaching in an Anti-Prophetic Age."[2] Like many, I am always in awe of the wisdom, profundity, and power with which Moss preaches, teaches, and lectures. That day was no different.

Moss spoke to the listening audience with crystal clear memory, depth of scholarly and theological application, and colloquial relevance from the Gospel according to Luke, chapter 4:18-21 and Isaiah 61:1-3.

Luke 4:18-21, KJV states:

> The Spirit of the Lord is upon me, because he hath anointed me to preach the gospel to the poor; he hath sent me to heal the brokenhearted, to preach deliverance to the captives, and recovering of sight to the blind, to set at liberty them that are bruised,
>
> To preach the acceptable year of the Lord.
>
> And he closed the book, and he gave it again to the minister, and sat down. And the eyes of all them that were in the synagogue were fastened on him.
>
> And he began to say unto them, This day is this scripture fulfilled in your ears.

In this passage, Jesus was quoting from the Hebrew Bible book of Isaiah, chapter 61:1-3, KJV. Those verses declare:

> The Spirit of the Lord God is upon me; because the Lord hath anointed me to preach good tidings unto the meek; he hath sent me to bind up the brokenhearted, to proclaim liberty to the captives, and the opening of the prison to them that are bound;
>
> To proclaim the acceptable year of the Lord, and the day of vengeance of our God; to comfort all that mourn;
>
> To appoint unto them that mourn in Zion, to give unto them beauty for ashes, the oil of joy for mourning, the garment of praise for the spirit of heaviness; that they might be called trees of righteousness, the planting of the Lord, that he might be glorified.

Moss used these passages as the background for his lecture. He emphasized that Jesus' sermon was short, convicting, and timeless. The religious leaders were angered most by Jesus' audacious proclamation, "Today, this scripture is fulfilled in your hearing," for in so doing, Jesus was declaring himself to be the fulfillment of the Hebrew Bible's prophesy of the coming Messiah.

According to Moss's explanation of the text, the phrase, "The Spirit of the Lord is upon me because he has anointed me to preach the Gospel," was theological. The next phrase, "to the poor," is economical, while "to set the captives free" is political. You cannot preach the whole gospel without being political.

Throughout the lecture, Otis Moss gave several examples to support his assertions. He described a poster used by the Poor People's Campaign with Martin Luther King Jr. in the center surrounded by poor people of all ethnicities. That was the message of the campaign. Poverty impacts people of all cultures, skin colors, and nationalities. We have a responsibility to work toward the eradication of poverty in America.

In America, we have been desensitized to poverty on many levels. We accept teachings that lead us to despise the poor. We look the other way when we see images of the impoverished that are brutal and dehumanizing. We ignore the methods used to teach us to hate and fear the poor, based upon our conditioning. We deny that there are long-established systems to perpetuate conditions of poverty across our nation. After all of that, we then feel licensed to kill them. Quoting Ghandi, Moss continued, "God has given us enough in the universe for our need but not for our greed." The sin is in the distribution.

Jesus proclaimed that he was sent to give sight to the blind. Moss reasoned that this emphasized Jesus' concern not only for the spiritual, but for physical, sociological, and educational liberation. Moss explained further that blindness burns books and worships dictators. He went on to unpack, "To proclaim the year of the Lord, or to proclaim the year of Jubilee." During the year of Jubilee every fifty years, slaves were set free, and debts were canceled. Moss concluded his lecture by declaring that Jesus came not for liberation to happen every fifty years, but rather to declare liberation RIGHT NOW!

At the Heart of Jesus' Words Is the Concept of Identity

Merriam-Webster defines identity as: 1a: "the distinguishing character or personality of an individual;" 3b: "sameness in all that constitutes the objective reality of a thing."[3] Jesus' prayer as presented in the Message version of the Bible clearly articulates Jesus' acknowledgment of his and his disciples' different identities, a holy identity. Specifically, they were hated for not joining the world's ways. Furthermore, they are not defined by the world. Ultimately, Jesus prays in this prayer that his disciples would be made holy, consecrated by God's word, the consecrating truth. He ends his prayer by saying, **"I'm consecrating myself for their sakes, so they'll be truth-consecrated in their mission."** To be consecrated means to be set apart for a special purpose. Jesus' disciples should be identified as those whose mission is to embody the transcendent love of Christ. This love is transcendent because it is higher, better, and stronger than the fake semblance of connections the world offers. God's love is unconditional. It is sacrificial in nature. It is grace-filled. It is divine.

> A new command I give you: Love one another. As I have loved you, so you must love one another. By this everyone will know that you are my disciples, if you love one another. —John 13:34-35

The profundity of this closing prayer statement should not be underestimated. Jesus wanted his disciples to be internally and externally governed by God's word, with a mission-mindedness that embodied God's truth, clothed in God's love and not the world's whims and dictates. Throughout Jesus' earthly ministry, he painstakingly exhibited what it meant to be "the word made flesh dwelling among us" (John 1:14). Jesus, at every turn, taught his disciples the clear distinction between the ways of the world, often exemplified by the religious leaders' hypocrisy and the mercy, grace, love, and empowerment God offered. Jesus offered a ministry of empowerment. He often asked those suffering from various conditions, "Wilt thou be made whole?" In the common vernacular, we might paraphrase, "Do you want to get well?" His words were empowering because the healing came not as something done *to them* but as something done *with them*. In each instance, the individual had a part to play. "Take up your bed and walk. Stretch forth your hand. Your faith has made you whole. Open the door, and I will come in. Cast your net over the side of the boat."

Through word and deed, Jesus taught us what partnership with God looks like. He showed us what it really means to engage, lift, and help people to stand, grow, and thrive. Jesus was not only concerned with soul salvation but with helping people to be made whole on "this side of the Jordan." When people have been put down enough, passed by enough, or denied access and opportunity enough, they often develop a situational identity. In other words, they begin to identify themselves, not as *who* they are, but rather by *what* people call them and *how* people treat them. Many embraced identities that were bound by negative descriptors: beggar, sinful woman, leper, whore, uncircumcised gentile, tax collector, etc. Jesus, however, acknowledged and affirmed their humanity. We find an example of this in Luke.

Jesus Heals a Crippled Woman on the Sabbath

> On a Sabbath Jesus was teaching in one of the synagogues, and a woman was there who had been crippled by a spirit for eighteen years. She was bent over

> and could not straighten up at all. When Jesus saw her, he called her forward and said to her, "Woman, you are set free from your infirmity." Then he put his hands on her, and immediately she straightened up and praised God.
>
> Indignant because Jesus had healed on the Sabbath, the synagogue leader said to the people, "There are six days for work. So come and be healed on those days, not on the Sabbath."
>
> The Lord answered him, "You hypocrites! Doesn't each of you on the Sabbath untie your ox or donkey from the stall and lead it out to give it water? Then should not this woman, a daughter of Abraham, whom Satan has kept bound for eighteen long years, be set free on the Sabbath day from what bound her?"—Luke 13:10-16

As the Pharisees indignantly called out Jesus for healing a severely infirmed woman on the Sabbath, Jesus took them to task, confronting their hypocrisy by asking them if they wouldn't give a thirsty animal a drink of water on the Sabbath? At the same time, Jesus highly honored this woman by calling her a "daughter of Abraham" (the most revered patriarch in the Jewish tradition), calling her forward, inviting her to be healed, touching her, and teaching the people what God's love really looks like!

While Jesus showed compassion, many religious leaders showed no care for the people. They took advantage of their desire to get closer to God by demanding that they follow traditions and excessive laws that God did not require. They were more concerned with *appearing* righteous than with *being* righteous. Jesus called them "whitewashed sepulchers" filled with dead men's bones (Matthew 23:27, KJV). Jesus harshly condemned the religious leaders for their actions and admonished his followers to reject their ways:

> For I tell you that unless your righteousness surpasses that of the Pharisees and the teachers of the law, you will certainly not enter the kingdom of heaven.
> —Matthew 5:20
>
> While all the people were listening, Jesus said to his disciples, "Beware of the teachers of the law. They like to walk around in flowing robes and love to be greeted with respect in the marketplaces and have the most important seats in the synagogues and the places of honor at banquets. They devour widows' houses and for a show make lengthy prayers. These men will be punished most severely."
> —Luke 20:45-47

Bad Theology, Identity Politics, and Power Structures

Women, children, people of color, and the poor have all been victims of systems developed and perpetuated by bad theology. America was built upon racist and sexist foundations. Misinterpretations of scripture were used to oppress and abuse women and children, dehumanize people of color, and blame the poor for their impoverished conditions. Below are a few examples of scriptures taken out of context and used to keep the powerful in power.

The Oppression and Demonization of Women

Women are blamed for the fall of humanity (Eve–Genesis 3:1-13).

Women are portrayed as sexual predators (Lot's daughters–Genesis 19:30-36; Delilah–Judges 16; Solomon's wives–1 Kings 11).

Women are depicted as deceitful and untrustworthy (Potiphar's wife–Genesis 39:7-20).

Women are suspected of fornication or adultery (Scriptures concerning sexual improprieties committed by women–Deuteronomy 22:13-21; Numbers 5:11-31).

Women are silenced for stepping out of their place in the church (1 Timothy 2:11-14).

In the above scriptures, we find the stories of women who have been demonized through the misinterpretation of scripture. Eve, the mother of humanity; Delilah, the temptress who lured Samson; and Lot's daughters, who got their father drunk and then slept with him to preserve their family line. Next, we see the pagan wives of Solomon, who turned his heart away from the Lord; the unnamed wife of Potiphar (the captain of Pharoah's guard), who tried to tempt Joseph to sleep with her, and several other scriptures that deal with women who have committed sexual indiscretions and are too outspoken in the church. A quick glance at these descriptions reveals that the men involved in each of these cases do not carry the weight of mischaracterizing ALL men across the human spectrum! This burden is only laid upon the backs of women.

Nobody mentions the disobedience of Adam; the repeated, foolish, arrogant, undisciplined behaviors of Judge Samson; the drunken state of Lot; the unbridled sexual exploits of Solomon; and the possibility that Potiphar (there is controversy as to whether the original texts support this idea; however, some commentators support it) was a eunuch.[4]

Though not justifiable, if her husband was indeed a eunuch, no consideration is given to the possibility that Potiphar's wife was a young woman, given (literally) to a man who could not provide her with children or satisfy her desires. When other passages of scripture concerning women committing adultery or fornication are used to characterize women as temptresses, little to no attention is given to the men with whom they commit the sinful acts.

Bad Theology Promotes Abuse, Poverty, and Death Among Women and Children

The patriarchy uses mischaracterizations like these to keep women down, to justify keeping them under subjection to men, and to create excuses for why women should not be given authority. Although American society has come a long way from "the rule of thumb," a British and American law that allowed husbands to discipline their wives and children with rods that were not larger than their thumb,[5] domestic violence is still a leading cause of medical injuries and death for women in America.

According to the National Library of Medicine, "Two intersecting public health crises in the US threaten women's health, safety, and equality: Intimate partner violence (IPV) and gun violence. More than half of female homicide victims are killed by a current or former male intimate partner, and 96 percent of murder-suicide victims are female. Firearms are used in more than 50 percent of these IPV-related homicides."[6]

When men believe that they are endowed by God with the right to rule over, subjugate, and dominate women, abuse and oppression are inevitable. In current-day America, women certainly have many more rights and opportunities than women in other countries around the world. Women in the US are free to choose their own husbands. Women have the right to vote, obtain an education, work outside of the home, and hold positions in the government, in the community, and in any number of sectors and arenas. Having said that, however, the United States of America remains one of only a few leading nations that has never elected a woman president.

Patriarchy leads to poverty among women. Sociologist Carolyn Aragao concluded that the pay gap between women and men in the United States continues to persist. Based upon a Pew Research Center analysis, women earned approximately 84 percent of men's earnings, when comparing the median hourly wages of both full-time and part-time employees. This analysis shows that women would need to work an extra forty-two days to match what men earned in 2020.[7] The wage gap has improved but has not been eliminated for younger workers. Young women between the ages of twenty-five and thirty-four earned ninety-three cents per dollar compared to young men in the same age group.[8]

According to the National Women's Law Center,[9] approximately 15.5 million women aged eighteen or older were impoverished in 2022. When broken down by race, poverty was particularly high among women of color: Black women (16.6 percent) and Latinas (16.8 percent). Women comprise six in ten of the elderly living in poverty.[10] One can deduce that ignorance, sexism, racism, and patriarchal structures continue to maintain abusive and economically oppressive systems, seriously impacting the lives of women and children in America.

Women across the US continue to experience high levels of poverty in general. In particular, female heads of households; Black, Latina, Asian, Native, and white, non-Hispanic women; the elderly; and children experienced the highest levels of poverty in the states of Kentucky, West Virginia, Louisiana, Mississippi, and Alabama (40-49 percent), according to NWLCA, based upon the 2023 US Census Bureau. Bad theology has also been used as a weapon of oppression against Indigenous and Black people.

Oppression and Dehumanization of Indigenous and Black People: Identity Politics in America

Scriptures Used to Justify Racism, Slavery, and Genocide

Over the years, increasing numbers of people have been made aware of the misinterpretations of scripture to justify the American slavery system. Following are a few examples:

SLAVES ARE ADMONISHED TO OBEY THEIR MASTERS IN EPHESIANS 6:5-7; COLOSSIANS 3:22.

In the book of Philemon, Paul writes to Philemon to receive his former slave as a Christian brother. This book was misused to encourage runaway slaves to return back to their slave owners.

THE CURSE OF HAM IS DESCRIBED IN GENESIS 9:18-27.

This passage served as a primary go-to scripture for the enslaving of Black people. After the flood (Genesis 6:9-9:17), Noah began drinking one day to the point where he became drunk. During his state of inebriation, the scripture says that he was found naked by his son Ham. Alarmed, Ham went and told his brothers Shem and Japheth, who, rather than looking upon their naked father, brought a garment and walked backward to cover their father's nakedness. As a result, Ham (Canan) was cursed for not having the same kind of sensitivity. Used to show God's endorsement of the cruel and unusual practice of slavery, the following verses, in particular, cultivated a perceived justifiable basis for using human beings as beasts of burden.

WHEN NOAH AWOKE FROM HIS WINE AND FOUND OUT WHAT HIS YOUNGEST SON HAD DONE TO HIM, HE SAID,

"Cursed be Canaan!
The lowest of slaves
will he be to his brothers."
He also said,
"Praise be to the LORD, the God of Shem!
May Canaan be the slave of Shem.
May God extend Japheth's territory;
may Japheth live in the tents of Shem,
and may Canaan be the slave of Japheth." (Genesis 9:24-27)

Slavery was not unique in the ancient world. People were commonly made slaves when their nation was conquered by another nation. Often, people were enslaved by their own people (ethnicity). For example, Greeks would enslave people who were perceived as uncultured and barbaric. The Hebrew Bible book of Deuteronomy discusses the treatment of persons who sold themselves to pay a debt. Their time of service was to be limited to seven years unless they desired to stay with their master for life (Deuteronomy 15). Both Christians and Muslims during the Middle Ages enslaved people who may have been considered pagan or godless.[11] In these contexts, slaves were not necessarily kept as slaves for life. Their children were not destined to be slaves. They could interact and socialize with others who were not slaves. In some situations, they could even earn or purchase their freedom, as in the case of indentured servants.[12]

The Trans-Atlantic Slave Trade of the 1500s ushered in a new kind of enslavement based upon institutionalized racism. Specifically, Black Africans were chosen to be the slaves and white Europeans slave owners.[13] The Curse of Ham theory worked well for their agenda. It provided to them a plausible justification, divinely ordained, to subjugate Black people (identified as descendants of Ham) to European/white ownership and rule.

Prior to this time, the concept of race as we know it was non-existent. People previously classified each other based on their ethnicity (culture or geographic origins). The concept of race is a social construct, an idea or body of ideas that have been created and accepted by a society. The term "race" was first recorded between 1490 and 1500 and was adopted into English from the Italian term *razza*, translated as "kind, breed, lineage."[14]

A shift occurred, however, during the 1700s as European colonialism emerged. The term changed from a form similar to ethnicity to a power-packed characterization of human beings into social hierarchical structures. To augment this new understanding in society, eighteenth and nineteenth century anthropologists, physiologists, and foremost thinkers of the day spread false claims that a person's race determined their intellectual abilities, brain size, moral character, and capabilities.[15] Some argue that this term was used initially among the Spanish (*raza*) with an original usage similar to the origins described above. Professor Anna Maria Gomez-Bravo theorizes that in the 1400s the Church and the Spanish monarchy joined forces to expand institutionalized racism to form a unified "Christian state," and undergird capitalist endeavors.[16] This argument seems accurate when viewed within the context of the oppression of indigenous people.

Race became the barometer by which Europeans determined human intelligence, worth, and societal classification. In addition to being ignorant and unethical, using skin color to make these determinations is fundamentally flawed, as skin tone is only a measure of the amount of melanin (pigmentation) a person has in their skin due to genetics.

Racist white religious academics disseminated false ideologies in churches, schools, homes, and society. Educational consultant L. Richard Bradley identified a variety of centuries-old writings that bolstered convenient arguments for skin tone and slavery.[17] For example, Bradley highlights Josiah Priest's explanation of the Curse of Ham in his 1853 book, *Bible Defense of Slavery*. Priest asserted that Noah's son Ham was somehow born "Black," while his brothers, from the same mother, were born white.[18] Therefore, Ham was preordained by God to be subjugated to his white brothers through slavery. As ridiculous as this notion appears, this argument and many similar ones proved exceedingly advantageous for those anxious to use Black bodies as chattel.

Scriptures Used to Oppress and Abuse Indigenous People

Knowledge of the use of scripture to rob Indigenous peoples of their lands may not be as well explored. What has been explored more extensively over the last few decades are the atrocities committed by the US government to force indigenous peoples off their land, change their names, reform their language, abandon their religious practices, and assimilate to white Christian belief systems.[19] Native American communities in general and their children in particular have experienced horrific abuses. Documentaries have been written that have uncovered these atrocities. Less has been explored concerning the scriptures used to oppress, disenfranchise, and abuse Indigenous peoples.

In 1862, the governor of Minnesota used Genesis 4:10 to justify killing Indigenous peoples in the Dakotas.[20] The scripture references God confronting Cain, the brother of Abel, after Cain killed his brother in the field. The scripture states,

> The Lord said, "What have you done? Listen! Your brother's blood cries out to me from the ground" (Genesis 4:10).

When Europeans tried to invade and steal land from the Dakotas, they rightly defended themselves and their land. White men died. In the eyes of the Minnesota Legislature, before whom the governor spoke, the people of Dakota were savages. They had no right to the land that they had lived on for thousands of years. The racists' ears heard the blood of the slaughtered white men crying out for revenge. Consequently, justice had to be done. Genocide and a land grab were the answer! Genesis 1:28 was another verse used to rob Native Americans of their lands in the Dakotas:

> God blessed them and said to them, "Be fruitful and increase in number; fill the earth and subdue it. Rule over the fish in the sea and the birds in the sky and over every living creature that moves on the ground" (Genesis 1:28).

Chris Mato Nunpa, member of the Pezihuta Zizi community and Bible scholar, specializes in the study of theology and the genocide, land theft, and religious suppression of Native

American people, especially the Dakota people in Minnesota. Mato Nunpa states:

> The "subdue the earth" notion helped provide the rationale for stealing Dakota lands, for removing Dakota people from their ancient homelands. This idea was expounded on by white supremacist Charles Bryant who said of the Dakota-US War of 1862 that it was "a conflict of knowledge with ignorance of right with wrong." Since the Dakota did not obey the injunction to subdue the earth, they were in the wrongful possession of a continent required by the superior right of the white man.[21]

Professor Robert Craig, in his article "Christianity and Empire: A Case Study of American Protestant Colonialism and Native Americans," unpacks the many travesties committed by Christian missionaries among Indigenous people. Quoting George Tinker, Craig calls the missionaries "partners in genocide and guilty of complicity in the destruction of Indian cultures and tribal social structures."[22] Craig further analyzes the tools of imperialism and colonialism in the development of the history of the United States and US Christianity. He states that Euro-Americans have cultivated a language that dominates their psychosocial processes, whether speaking theologically, politically, or socioeconomically—a language that inhibits their ability to see themselves as they truly are. Quoting the words of Clifford Geertz, Craig writes that dominant culture peoples' "frames of meaning—how they perceive themselves—are subject to systematic distortion." Their distorted perceptions of themselves as "Christian" and Indigenous people as "savages," cultivated within them a false identity that God had commissioned them to either save (through "church talk") or kill those who refuse to convert.[23]

In both instances of the enslavement of Black Africans and the oppression and abuse of Native Americans, the Bible was used to justify the dehumanizing practices. God had nothing to do with their evil engagements. In fact, God abhors oppression, abuse, and false piety:

> Is this the kind of fast I have chosen,
> only a day for people to humble themselves?
> Is it only for bowing one's head like a reed
> and for lying in sackcloth and ashes?
> Is that what you call a fast,
> a day acceptable to the Lord?
> "Is not this the kind of fasting I have chosen:
> to loose the chains of injustice
> and untie the cords of the yoke,
> to set the oppressed free
> and break every yoke?
> Is it not to share your food with the hungry
> and to provide the poor wanderer with shelter—
> when you see the naked, to clothe them,
> and not to turn away from your own flesh and blood? (Isaiah 58:5-7)

Identity Politics

In America, some argue that our nation has experienced a broad shift from economy-based political affiliations to identity-based politics. *The Oxford English Dictionary* defines *identity politics* as, "a tendency for people of a particular religion, ethnic group, social background, etc., to form exclusive political alliances, moving away from traditional broad-based party politics."[24]

In his book *Age of Revolutions: Progress and backlash from 1600 to the present*, journalist Fareed Zakaria asserts that the 1960s Civil Rights era ushered in a new political paradigm. Zakaria states:

> Almost every contemporary social movement, from #MeToo and Black Lives Matter to the conservative fight against critical race theory, is wrestling with the ideas that were first articulated in that decade. Where politics was once overwhelmingly shaped by economics, politics today is being transformed by identity.[25]

I argue that identity politics were happening long before the Civil Rights Movement in the 1960s. The United States Declaration of Independence, signed by five white men in 1776, rests within the hallowed walls of the Rotunda at the National Archives Museum. This historical American document shamelessly identifies Native Americans as "merciless Indian Savages, whose known rule of warfare, is an undistinguished destruction of all ages, sexes and conditions."[26]

When the Spaniard Christopher Columbus landed on the shores of the Americas in 1492, he erroneously labeled the Indigenous people "Indians" because he believed he had landed in "the Indies," or India of Southeast Asia, his intended destination.[27] To advance the occupation and colonization of his "discovery" of the New World, Columbus needed political and religious backing. He needed to characterize the persons living on the land as less than human, brute savages, and a danger to the Europeans. Therefore, he sought the authority to take over the land. The pope in Rome, head of the Western Christian Church, honored his request.[28] The pope gave Columbus the authority to seize the land, colonize, and kill the current occupants, as they were not Christians. The claim was that God had given them the okay to commit genocide and enslavement because the Indigenous people were idolatrous, paganistic, and soulless.

The Doctrine of Discovery, the edict issued by Pope Alexander VI on May 4, 1493, made Spain's dominance of the New World legal. Called the Papal Bull *Inter Caetera,* the document claimed that any land not inhabited by Christians was allowed to be claimed by the Catholic Church. Additionally, the Christian faith was to be imposed upon people throughout the land, so that "the health of souls be cared for and that barbarous nations be overthrown and brought to the faith itself."[29] The Discovery Doctrine ultimately served as the foundation for European takeovers in the Americas. The United States followed suit to engage in its western expansion.[30]

Similarly, when people were brutally captured from the continent of Africa and enslaved during the Trans-Atlantic Slave Trade, the slavers determined it was necessary to characterize the slaves as less than human, ignorant, animalistic beings that needed to be completely controlled. African slaves were also stripped of their language, their culture, their religion, and their families. They were brought to a strange and cruel land that called itself Christian. Like Indigenous Americans, Black people were given a peculiar designation in America's historical documents. Article One, Section Two of the United States Constitution stated that enslaved individuals would be counted as three-fifths of a free person to determine congressional representation. Known as the Three-fifths Compromise (1787), delegates from the Northern and Southern states struck a deal to consider slaves as three-fifths of a person to determine taxation and representation in the United States House of Representatives.[31]

In 1830, President Andrew Jackson (whose face continues to be seen on the twenty-dollar bill) signed the Indian Removal Act, authorizing the government takeover of Indigenous-owned lands by forcibly removing Native peoples. Historical records indicate that thousands of Cherokee people later died on what is known as the "Trail of Tears." Reportedly, President Jackson declared that the forced removal of the Indigenous people would "incalculably strengthen the southwestern frontier," enabling states like Alabama and Mississippi to "advance rapidly in population, wealth, and power."[32]

For both Native Americans and Black people, false identities were imposed upon them—identities that had no resemblance to their culture, spirituality, their familial traditions, nor their understandings of the Holy One. They were branded with identities that would shape the realities of their existence in America—realities that were cruel, unusual, and altering. These same false identities massively influence how each group is characterized, systemically oppressed, disenfranchised, and deliberately penalized (both figuratively and literally through American prison systems) in America. False piety and power were used to rationalize murders of mind, body, and spirit. In some instances, the mischaracterizations were so overwhelming, that even those made to swallow the lies about themselves begin to embrace the ugliness. In the words of Toni Morrison, "We acquiesce and say the victim had no right to live."[33]

False Piety, Power, and Poverty

> Whoever oppresses the poor shows contempt for their Maker, but whoever is kind to the needy honors God. (Proverbs 14:31)
>
> I like your Christ, I do not like your Christians. Your Christians are so unlike your Christ.
>
> —Mahatma Gandhi[34]

Sometimes, false piety is at play, and the perpetrator is unaware. One of the most effective tools of the powerful is to persuade the oppressed to ignore the systems that have promoted and produced their impoverished conditions. In *White Rural Rage: The Threat to American Democracy,* Tom Schaller and Paul Waldman unpack the cultivation of resentment, xenophobia (otherism), misguided faith, and extreme right-wing politics among impoverished white rural Americans. Schaller and Waldman suggest that white rural Americans, embattled by the loss of income due to manufacturing jobs being sent overseas, the dismantling of unions, technological advancement, and environmental policy changes (e.g., moving from coal production to clean energy) positioned them to become prime targets for politicians peddling conspiracy theories.[35] They describe the plan as:

> Keep rural Americans bitter, and they'll be an easily manipulated force of destruction when democracy doesn't produce proper results. The worse rural Americans feel, the better this plan works.[36]

Further, the authors assert that powerful political leaders, appearing godly and American, convince poor rural whites and even lower middle-class whites that at the root of all their problems are lazy people of color, illegal immigrants, and ungodly far-left politicians. They somehow convince their listeners that God has chosen them for such a time as this. They weave into this deceitful rhetoric that the only way to fight back against the forces of evil is to elect even more conservative politicians who claim to love the Lord and understand their struggles. The right wing's uncanny ability to persuade their audiences to ignore hard facts: no new jobs brought to their communities, no expansion of healthcare benefits for their families, no increase in their wages, no answers for their poor educational structures, etc., is mind-boggling. Their audience remains faithful to following their political guidance.

This manipulation of vulnerable people is not magical or new. This strategy can be traced back to the Antebellum South. During slavery, poor white people struggled to survive. They were up against an economy of slavery that stripped them of employment opportunities. Slave labor was free. Everything from picking cotton; raising, feeding, and slaughtering livestock; cleaning barns, sheds, houses; chopping wood; blacksmith work; and more—ALL these things took away employment opportunities from poor white people.

In the book *Masterless Men: Poor Whites and Slavery in the Antebellum South*, Keri Leigh Merritt powerfully delineates the methods used by upper-class whites to keep slaves and poor whites at odds against one another. Merritt posits that the vestiges of the carefully crafted divisions between black slaves and poor or working-class whites continue to haunt American society.[37] Quoting a leading populist speaker in the late 1800s, Georgian Tom Watson, Merritt (concerning stoked divisions between enslaved Blacks and poor, working-class whites) shares:

> You are kept apart that you may be separately fleeced of your earnings. You are made to hate each other because upon that hatred is rested the keystone of the arch of financial despotism which enslaves you both. You are deceived and blinded that you may not see how this race antagonism perpetuates a monetary system which beggars both.[38]

Many examples of poor whites and enslaved Blacks, banding together to remedy their torturous conditions, have been deliberately written out of history. During the mid to late 1800s, slave traders pushed hundreds of thousands of slaves into the Deep South. Georgia, Alabama, and Mississippi, experiencing this influx of free labor, displaced large numbers of poor and working-class whites. Poor whites did not own land or slaves. Their skills were no longer needed. They were either unemployed or underemployed. For all these reasons, the institution of slavery was of no benefit to them.[39]

In the article "Keeping Poor Whites and Blacks Apart: A Southern Tradition," Merritt explains how poor, working-class whites and Black people engaged in a variety of social and political activities together. Poor whites and Blacks were both blocked from participating in the formal Southern economy. To compensate for this abominable injustice, they created their own economy, an underground economy where they traded various items (liquor, food, and services) for their appeasement and survival.[40]

Recognizing the power and threat of these newly formed alliances, wealthy, upper-class whites in general, and plantation/slave owners in particular, implemented a variety of strategies to stop the brewing rebellion. White people who traded resources with slaves were severely punished. If caught, they would be stripped, beaten, lynched, etc., at the hands of slaves made to do so by their slave masters. In addition to beatings and lynchings, so-called vigilance committees (often comprised of lawmakers) were formed, along with policies to ensure the separation between the races.[41]

Strict laws were enforced by local and state government officials to use both the penal system, through jailing individuals without just cause and vigilante tactics to control poor, working-class whites free and enslaved Blacks through acts of terrorism (e.g., night riders and Ku Klux Klan–like measures); and fear. Yet all these strategies lacked the power to completely break the recognition of their mutual circumstances of oppression. Something dastardlier was needed in order to do so.

Not lacking in ingenuity (if one could call it that), wealthy whites employed several strategies to create both psychological and theological barriers between poor, working-class whites and Blacks. They would offer some financial relief to lower-class whites by creating low-level positions (e.g., slave overseers, couriers, shopkeepers, guards, jailers, etc.), reward them for keeping an eye on slaves, ensuring that they would not run away, *and*, maybe the most effective tactic of all, teach them that by divine order, they were meant to lord over Black people (as in the "Curse of Ham" discussion). The concept of white superiority would become the cornerstone of racism and the perpetuation of systems of oppression—systems that continue to dominate American culture today.

In the book *Why Does Everything Have to Be About Race?*,[42] film producer and former aide to President Clinton Keith Boykin provides a chronological listing of events from 1526–2023, involving the use of race as a means to oppress people of color horrifically. He details their experiences of enslavement, seized lands, placement into prison camps, and designations as less than human. Boykin further explores other forms of unequal applications of the law that benefit white people, such as the recharacterization of an angry mob's attack on the US Capitol as patriots and families peacefully visiting the "People's House" with a "few bad actors." Boykin quotes Toni Morrison, who says, "The function of racism is distraction."[43] Indeed, the distraction playbook has been exceedingly successful. As discussed previously, many poor, working-class, and other-class whites during the Antebellum period and in today's America are distracted by a preponderance of misinformation peddled on local news and a variety of media outlets. People of color continue to be painted as the primary actors in violent crimes, as the drivers of a struggling economy due to their dependence upon welfare, and as the source of many of our country's woes.

Boykin invites his readers to consider how white supremacy and racism are used in general, and against Black people in particular, to distract the unsuspecting from the realities both these ideologies create. By erasing Black history, promoting the idea of white victimhood, denying Black oppression, and advancing myths about Black inferiority, white privilege and systems of oppression are left unchecked and flourishing.[44]

The reality of Boykin's assertions has taken shape in real time. Vice President J.D. Vance spewed vicious lies about Haitians fleeing turmoil and violence in Haiti who settled in Springfield, Ohio, during the election. The backstory behind this unfounded rumor was that since 2021, between 12,000 and 20,000 Haitians have settled in Springfield, a small, predominantly white, industrial community with about 60,000 people. While many had previously lived in South Florida, Boston, and New York, the area attracted them because of the lower cost of living and large numbers of employment opportunities. As a result, many Haitians have legally made Springfield their home.[45]

For employers and newcomers, this influx of new community members appeared to be a win-win situation. Employers were able to hire struggling immigrants for lower wages, and the workers could build a new life. So, what was the problem? Others in the community began to feel pushed out of jobs, overwhelmed by Black people with a funny accent, and angry over a broken immigration system. Fingers began pointing, not at the employers who did not offer competitive pay to the original residents, but rather to Black foreigners who appeared to be stealing their jobs.

Seeing this conflict as an opportunity to stoke divisions and bolster the Trumpian claim that the Biden Administration allowed massive amounts of illegal aliens to come into America, bringing drugs, crime, rapists, murderers, mentally ill, etc., poisoning the blood of America, then–vice presidential candidate J.D. Vance sprang into action. On social media and during news interviews, Vance spread wild, racist, and volatile lies that the Haitians in Springfield, Ohio, were stealing pets, including dogs, cats, and ducks, and eating them.[46]

While the people of Springfield may have other legitimate concerns about resources, living spaces, and major changes due to large numbers of new residents in their small community (approximately 15 percent of their total population), the mayor, city officials, and residents have all debunked Vance's false claims. Despite all contrary reports of Vance's outlandish statements, he continued to spew his xenophobic, racist, deplorable rhetoric.

As a result, the Haitian community expressed confusion and fear. Schools and hospitals received bomb threats. Children and adults expressed concerns about their safety. Innocent people are being attacked both verbally and, in some instances, physically. Vance co-opted the hate-filled storyline from white supremacists and neo-Nazi groups, known for marching through Springfield carrying swastika-emblazoned flags and protesting against Haitian immigrants. They fueled the rumor that pets began disappearing when the Haitians came to town.[47] This tragic story is a cautionary tale of how lies spread by political extremists can rain down devastating results upon innocent people, invoking otherisms and racist fears that stoke hatred and divisions to their advantage.

False Piety and Racism as Tools

In 2024, Stephen Ujlaki created the documentary, *Bad Faith: Christian Nationalism's Unholy War on Democracy*.[48] Film director, screenwriting professor, and former dean of Loyola Marymount University, Ujlaki, along with a host of historians, journalists, former members of the Trump administration, pastors, civil rights leaders, etc., unpack an unparalleled depth of strategy used to court, manipulate, and corral evangelicals into a formidable voting movement. The film features key players who spearheaded the underground machinery that meticulously weaved faith and political agendas together.

Special attention is given to Paul Weyrich, the chief mastermind of this political movement, and the founder of the Council for National Policy (CNP). The CNP offers anonymity and closed meetings for its members. Weyrich is credited with developing lucrative relationships with conservative evangelicals and the Republican Party. Along with evangelical pastor the late Jerry Falwell and influential Christian Network *700 Club* founder Pat Robinson, Weyrich helped to launch The Moral Majority, a political power bloc. The network reportedly had over 72,000 pastors at one time.

Weyrich would visit churches and preach to evangelical congregations about the evils of the Democratic Party liberals. He warned that if they were allowed to remain in power, America would be completely corrupted. This was not a fight against human beings, Weyrich posited. It was a fight against Satan himself. Pastors were encouraged to use sermons and Bible studies to drive this point home—a point that would compel parishioners to go to the ballot box and vote down tickets for Republicans.

While segregation had been used effectively in the Jim Crow South, it did not hold the same broad appeal across the nation. Therefore, they needed a galvanizing issue or two that would bring a multitude of evangelicals together to vote for conservative values. In the 1970s, Weyrich turned the spotlight on abortion and homosexuality. The pro-life movement was born. Radio programs like *Focus on the Family* with James Dobson, continuing promotions by Pat Robinson and Jerry Falwell, and thousands of conservative evangelists and pastors, Weyrich and the Republicans found the key that unlocked the votes needed to place and keep them in power for years to come. Through congressional seats, district and circuit courts, and ultimately the Supreme Court, political power would be wielded for generations.

Weyrich also asserted that only certain members of the populace should have the right to vote. In the film, he boldly and publicly states that the voting populace should go down. Conceivably, following the 1960s Civil Rights era Voting Rights Act, the Council for National Policy became the leading voice in creating systems of voter suppression. It is important to note that following slavery, the Thirteenth, Fourteenth, and Fifteenth Amendments to the Constitution were all written to provide a level of equality to Black people, giving them the rights of citizenship.[49]

After the assassination of President Abraham Lincoln in 1865, Lincoln's successor, President Andrew Johnson, was more concerned about states' rights than he was about granting rights to newly freed slaves. While he enforced the ratification of the Thirteenth Amendment (the abolishment of slavery in the US and its territories) in the Confederate states, Johnson allowed those same states to govern according to their own free will. He therefore sought to create policies that gave former Southern slave states the ability to enforce Black codes that denied free slaves the rights of citizenship, essentially keeping them, for all practical purposes, enslaved.[50]

Ironically, it was the Republican Party representatives who were outraged. In 1866, the Republican-led Congress passed the Civil Rights Bill, which further advanced the power of the Thirteenth Amendment, giving freed slaves the right to vote and live as equals among their white counterparts. In an attempt to keep the fragile North and South Union together, Johnson vetoed the bill. However, Congress rose to the occasion and sustained the necessary two-thirds majority to override a presidential veto.[51] It marked the first time in American history that Congress enacted a law despite the president's veto. Remembering the Party of Lincoln, a number of Black people remain Republicans today. Unfortunately, the Republicans of the Reconstruction era and those tethered to the movements currently under discussion are worlds apart.

The 1980s ushered in a wave of victories for conservative Republican leaders and evangelicals. The late President Ronald Reagan was identified as the standard bearer for the conservative cause. Pegged as a man of godly character, family values, and most importantly, pro-life, he was believed to be God's man for the country. His opponent, the late President Jimmy Carter, was characterized as an evil liberal who would destroy America with loose values, allowing vagrants and criminals to come into our clean, godly nation, and would turn our families away from the Lord. (Sound familiar?) Reagan employed the phrase "Let's Make America Great Again" during his rallies and political speeches. Reagan declared that if he were on a deserted island and could only have one book, it would be the Bible. Reagan stood with evangelicals and declared that he was pro-life (although he at least believed in exceptions for rape, incest, and the life of the mother).[52]

President Reagan was an answer to the conservative voters' prayers, or so they thought. Although they were initially enthralled with Reagan, the lovefest swiftly unraveled with his appointment of Judge Sandra Day O'Connor to the Supreme Court. She was the first woman appointed to the Court, who happened to be pro-choice. The evangelicals felt betrayed and therefore turned to other devices to promote their false piety and political agendas. Anne Nelson, in her book *Shadow Network: Media, Money, and the Secret Hub of the Radical Right*, discusses the process through which extreme conservative politics gained a foothold. Nelson unpacks the advancement of a concept known as Dominionism.[53] Dominionist theorists believe America is a Christian nation founded upon Christian principles. Christians (not all Christians, but primarily white, evangelical, conservative Christians) should lead and control every aspect of American Society. Specifically, they identify the Seven Mountains in their Watchman's Decree. They believe God has called and ordained them to be watchmen on the wall (taken from Ezekiel 33:1-6). They are to have dominion over each of the seven mountains: Family, Religion, Entertainment, Media, Education, Business, and Government.[54]

Paul Weyrich and another political strategist Ralph Reed, founder and chairman of the Faith and Freedom Coalition, banded together to court billionaire oil barrens, and other extraordinarily wealthy businessmen, such as the famous Koch brothers, to pour millions of dollars into the aforementioned conservative organizations for printing materials, funding events, holding workshops and training sessions. Many pastors, preachers, teachers, and evangelists who were a part of the evangelical political movement were rewarded with millions of dollars for their ministries and themselves.[55]

So-called evangelical megachurches played a role in their strategy. In one fell swoop, a megachurch pastor who literally influenced thousands of congregants both in person and online could yield just as many votes, potentially. In exchange for their influence, they received millions of dollars. They also agreed to invite Weyrich and Reed to their churches to conduct special events, teaching members how to use printed pamphlets and other materials and listing faith and family-friendly candidates to vote for in upcoming elections.[56]

In the meetings, church members were trained to identify conservative non-voters, provide them with materials highlighting what they believed to be at stake if liberals were to get into office, encourage them to register to vote, and provide them with suggestions of who would best serve their interests in office. The Family Research Council was given access to church directories and voter profiles, which they used to cross-reference and target individuals for their campaigns. According to the documentary, people were contacted between seven to twelve times each. A great many of these endeavors were funded by million and billionaire business tycoons.[57]

What was in it for the wealthy donors? This powerful, evangelical voting block would usher extreme conservatives into Congress that would vote for the elimination or at least a massive reduction of taxes for wealthy businesses, the dismantling of regulations meant to safeguard the nation's health and the environment, the busting up of unions that ensured fair wages, safe working conditions, and benefits. What did the wealthy donors get in exchange for their massive donations to these so-called Christian organizations? They gained the freedom to expand the earnings gap in America such that 1 percent of the nation holds approximately 90 percent of the wealth. They gained a Supreme Court that would turn back the clock on Affirmative Action policies, a woman's right to choose, healthcare coverage, and regulatory policies. They gained the ability to make billions of dollars off of weapons of war that were never meant for the civilian population, devastating drugs that produced massive amounts of opioid addictions, privatized schools that have wreaked havoc on our public school systems, as well as privatized prisons that use Black and Brown bodies as their chess pieces for who can win the highest bid for contracts.

Concerning the evangelical church members, either they did not care or did not understand fully that they were being used as a tool to place America on a trajectory that would spawn hatred, divisions, mass murders, xenophobia, misogyny, and all kinds of isms. Their false piety produced the opposite of what the Lord God declared pleased him—to do justly, to love mercy, and to walk humbly with God (Micah 6:8) to love God and to love our neighbors as ourselves (Matthew 22:36-40) that people would be able to identify the followers of Jesus by our love (John 13:35). They seemed to have forgotten that the love of money is the root of all evil (1 Timothy 6:10).

William Barber II, the renowned pastor and activist who founded the Poor People's Campaign and Yale's Center for Public Theology and Public Policy, said:

> Racism is not just about hating Black people. It is really, fundamentally about hating democracy, and racism becomes a tool for feeding the corporate greed of a few, who want an aristocracy, and nothing that leads to a democracy.[58]

We are seeing Barber's assessment of the end goal of racism play out in real time.

Jesus' prayer for his disciples as he faced crucifixion, declaring that they are *in* the world, but not *of* the world, leads us to a greater understanding of Jesus' heart for our lives. The light of Jesus' ministry provides a glaring contrast to false piety and everything it represents in today's culture. Through many examples, we can see strong correlations between the misinterpretation of the scriptures, patriarchy, racism, sexism, capitalism, and the oppression of specific groups of people (women, children, Black, Brown, Indigenous, and poor or working-class white people) in the church and society. The origins of the American concept of race, as well as specific examples of bad theology, identity politics, and power structures, have greatly influenced how we in America interact with each other.

In Chapter 3, we will discuss intersectionality theory. We will pay particular attention to the relationships between false piety, power, glass cliffs, and barriers in America.

Questions and Discussion Starters

At the beginning of this chapter, we considered two primary questions: (1) How is the false piety of religious leaders in Jesus' day similar to what we see happening in American society? (2) How have our identities been influenced and sometimes shaped by false piety, power, and politics?

Below are questions to help you contemplate, process, and share your thoughts.

1. Based upon Jesus' prayer for his disciples, how would you define a "holy identity"? How is that identity different from those cultivated by false piety and power?
2. Discuss ways that "bad faith" has contributed to our broken political system in America.
3. In your view, how has false piety and power influenced how we treat one another?
4. How can church and community come together to address systems (economic, mental health, educational, prison, etc.) that have produced historic injustices against Native American, Black, and Brown peoples in the United States?
5. List one thing that individuals and local groups can do to bring awareness to identity mischaracterizations and systems of oppression.

NOTES

1. Toni Morrison, *The Bluest Eye* (New York: Vintage Books, 1970), 206.
2. Otis Moss Jr., "Prophetic preaching in an anti-prophetic age," *Progressive National Baptist Convention, Compelling Preaching Series*, April 6, 2024, Olivet Institutional Baptist Church, Cleveland, Ohio.
3. "Identity," *Merriam-Webster*, n.d. https://www.merriam-webster.com/dictionary/identity#:~:text=identity-,noun,or%20personality%20of%20an%20individual.
4. Alan Aycock, "Potiphar's Wife: Prelude to a Structural Exegesis." *Man* 27, no. 3 (1992): 479–94. https://doi.org/10.2307/2803925;

Jepchumba Beckie & Chosefu Chemorion, "Revisiting the Character of Potiphar's Wife: A Narrative of Criticism of Genesis 39," *African Multidisciplinary Journal of Research* 6, No. 1 (2021): 1–18. ISSN 2518-2986.

5. United States Commission on Civil Rights, "Under the rule of thumb: Battered women and the administration of justice," *The Commission*, 1982, 1–2, https://www.nlm.nih.gov/exhibition/confrontingviolence/assets/transcripts/OB12012_200_dpi.pdf.

6. Elizabeth Tobin-Tyler, "Intimate Partner Violence, Firearm Injuries and Homicides: A Health Justice Approach to Two Intersecting Public Health Crises," *Journal of Law, Medicine, and Ethics* 5, No. 1 (2023): 64–76, doi: 10.1017/jme.2023.41. PMID: 37226755; PMCID: PMC10209983.

7. Carolina Aragao, "Gender Pay Gap in US Held Steady in 2020," *Pew Research Center*, March 1, 2023, https://www.pewresearch.org/fact-tank/2021/05/25/gender-pay-gap-facts.

8. Christine A. Smith, "Lived Experiences of Inequity of African American Women Leading Struggling, Nonprofit Organizations in the United States: A Phenomenological Study," Dissertation, Capella University, 2022, *ProQuest Dissertations Publishing*, 28964693.

9. National Women's Law Center, "Women in Poverty State by State," *National Women's Law Center,* October 3, 2024, https://nwlc.org/resource/women-in-poverty-state-by-state-2022/.

10. US Census Bureau, "National Poverty Rates Calculated by NWLC Based on US Census Bureau, Current Population Survey," *Annual Social and Economic Supplement*, 2023, https://www.census.gov/programs-surveys/cps.htm.

11. Robert Harms, "An Ancient Practice Transformed by the Arrival of Europeans Slavery existed in Africa long before Columbus, but the trans-Atlantic trade turned it into a very different institution." *Wall Street Journal,* September 20, 2019, https://www.wsj.com/articles/an-ancient-practice-transformed-by-the-arrival-of-europeans-11568993153.

12. The Smithsonian National Museum of African American History & Culture, "Talking about race," *Smithsonian*, n.d., https://nmaahc.si.edu/learn/talking-about-race/topics/historical-foundations-race.

13. Robert Harms, "An Ancient Practice Transformed by the Arrival of Europeans Slavery existed in Africa long before Columbus, but the trans-Atlantic trade turned it into a very different institution." *Wall Street Journal,* September 20, 2019, https://www.wsj.com/articles/an-ancient-practice-transformed-by-the-arrival-of-europeans-11568993153.

14. Alyssa Pereira, "Race vs. Ethnicity: Why these terms are so complex," *Dictionary.com*, July 31, 2020, https://www.dictionary.com/e/race-vs-ethnicity/.

15. Pereira, "Race vs. Ethnicity."

16. Ana M. Gomez-Bravo, "The Origins of Raza: Racializing Difference in Early Spanish," *Interfaces*, 2020, 7 No. 05, 64–114, DOI: 10.13130/interfaces-07-05.

17. L. Richard Bradley, "The Curse of Canaan and the American Negro," *Concordia Theological Monthly,* February 1, 1971, 42, No. 1, 10, https://scholar.csl.edu/ctm/vol42/iss1/10/.
18. Bradley, "The Curse of Canaan," 4.
19. Brenda J. Child, "Christianity was a major part of Indigenous boarding schools. Why that matters | Opinion," *Pennsylvania Capital-Star,* August 1, 2022, https://penncapital-star.com/commentary/christianity-was-a-major-part-of-indigenous-boarding-schools-why-that-matters-opinion/#:~:text=Cultural%20survival,through%20running%20away%20from%20school.
20. Amanda Anderson, "The Great Evil: Christianity, the Bible and the Native American Genocide," September 2, 2022, *Pioneer PBS,* https://www.pioneer.org/blogs/compass-stories/the-great-evil-christianity-the-bible-and-the-native-american-genocide/.
21. Anderson, "The Great Evil."
22. Robert Craig, "Christianity and Empire: A Case Study of American Protestant Colonialism and Native Americans," *American Indian Culture and Research Journal*, 21, No. 2, 3. https://escholarship.org/uc/item/5f29z35v.
23. Craig, "Christianity and Empire," 2.
24. "Oxford English Dictionary." Oed.com. 2025, https://www.oed.com/dictionary/identity-politics_n?tab=factsheet#140722645100.
25. Fareed Zakaria, *Age of Revolutions: Progress and Backlash from 1600 to the Present* (Random House, 2024), 217.
26. National Archives, "Declaration of Independence: A Transcription," *The Declaration of Independence,* n.d., https://www.archives.gov/founding-docs/declaration-transcript.
27. Elizabeth Prine Pauls, "Tribal Nomenclature: American Indian, Native American, and First Nation," *Encyclopedia Britannica,* January 17, 2008, https://www.britannica.com/topic/Tribal-Nomenclature-American-Indian-Native-American-and-First-Nation-1386025.
28. Rosie Dawson, "The 'White Christian Problem':" The Doctrine of Discovery That Encouraged Enslavement and Lynchings," *Religion Media Centre,* September 11, 2023, https://religionmediacentre.org.uk/news/the-white-christian-problem-the-doctrine-of-discovery-that-encouraged-enslavement-and-lynchings/.
29. The Gilder Lehrman Institute of American History, "The Doctrine of Discovery, 1493," *PBS Thirteen: The Making of America*, 2004, https://www.gilderlehrman.org/history-resources/spotlight-primary-source/doctrine-discovery-1493, https://www.thirteen.org/wnet/slavery/experience/legal/docs2.html.
29. Dawson, "The 'White Christian Problem.'"
31. The Gilder Lehrman Institute of American History, "The Slave Experience: Legal Rights & Government: The US Constitution, Article 1. Section 2. The 'Three-Fifths Clause,' Ratified, 1788," *PBS Thirteen: Slavery and The Making of America*, 2004, https://www.thirteen.org/wnet/slavery/experience/legal/docs2.html.

31. Keith Boykin, *Why Does Everything Have to Be About Race?* (Bold Type Books, 2024), x.

32. National Archives, "President Andrew Jackson's Message to Congress 'On Indian Removal' 1830," *Milestone Documents*, n.d., https://www.archives.gov/milestone-documents/jacksons-message-to-congress-on-indian-removal#:~:text=By%20the%20end%20of%20Jackson's,what%20later%20became%20eastern%20Oklahoma.

33. Toni Morrison, *The Bluest Eye* (Holt, Reinhart, and Winston, 1970), 206.

34. Mahatma Gandhi, "I like your Christ, I do not like your Christians. Your Christians are so unlike your Christ," *Goodreads*, n.d., https://www.goodreads.com/quotes/22155-i-like-your-christ-i-do-not-like-your-christians.

35. Tom Schaller and Paul Waldman, *White Rural Rage: The Threat to American Democracy* (Penguin Random House, 2024).

36. Schaller and Waldman, *White Rural Rage,* 4.

37. Keri Leigh Merrit, *Masterless Men: Poor Whites and Slavery in the Antebellum South* (Cambridge: Cambridge University Press, 2017), https://doi.org/10.1017/9781316875568.

38. Thomas E. Watson, "The Negro Question in the South," *The Arena,* VI (October 1892): 540–550, https://msuweb.montclair.edu/~furrg/spl/tomwatson.html.

39. Keri Leigh Merrit, "Keeping Poor Whites and Blacks Apart: A Southern Tradition." The Bitter Southerner Blog, 2023, https://bittersoutherner.com/from-the-southern-perspective/miscellany/what-you-dont-know-about-the-south.

40. Merrit, para 10.

41. Merrit, para 13.

43. Keith Boykin, *Why Does Everything Have to Be About Race?* (New York: Bold Type Books, 2024), x.

44. Boykin, 2.

45. Miriam Jordan, "Why thousands of Haitians have settled in Springfield, Ohio," *New York Times,* September 18, 2024, https://www.nytimes.com/2024/09/14/us/haitian-migrants-springfield-ohio.html?auth=login-google1tap&login=google1tap.

46. Huo Jingnan and Jasmine Garsd, "JD Vance spread debunked claims about Haitian immigrants eating pets," in "Special Series: Untangling Misinformation," *NPR,* September 10, 2024, https://www.npr.org/2024/09/10/nx-s1-5107320/jd-vance-springfield-ohio-haitians-pets.

47. Jingnan and Garsd, para. 4.

48. Stephen Ujlaki, Co-Director, Christopher Jones, *Bad Faith: Christian Nationalism's Unholy War on Democracy*, San Francisco: The Film Sales Company, 2024, https://www.badfaithdocumentary.com/about.

49. Sarah Pruitt, "When did African Americans Actually Get the Right to Vote?" *History,* October 8, 2024, https://www.history.com/news/african-american-voting-right-15th-amendment.

50. Pruitt, para. 3 and 4.

51. Pruitt, para. 5.
52. Bill Peterson, 1983. "Reagan Backs Bill to Prohibit Abortion Funds." *Washington Post*, January 22, 1983, https://www.washingtonpost.com/archive/politics/1983/01/22/reagan-backs-bill-to-prohibit-abortion-funds/d6f3e29e-0f90-45da-8368-5fb98a5d73f1/.
53. Anne Nelson, *Shadow Network: Media, Money, and the Secret Hub of the Radical Right* (Bloomsbury Publishing, 2019).
54. Nelson, 133.
55. Ujlaki, *Bad Faith*.
56. Nelson, *Shadow Network*, 90-91; Ujlaki, *Bad Faith*.
57. Ujlaki, *Bad Faith*.
58. Ujlaki, *Bad Faith*.

CHAPTER 3

Barriers and Glass Cliffs: How Race, Gender, and Class Intersect to Expand Oppression

These days, I start with what it's not, because there has been distortion. It's not identity politics on steroids. It is not a mechanism to turn white men into the new pariahs. It's basically a lens, a prism, for seeing the way in which various forms of inequality often operate together and exacerbate each other. We tend to talk about race inequality as separate from inequality based on gender, class, sexuality or immigrant status. What's often missing is how some people are subject to all of these, and the experience is not just the sum of its parts. —KIMBERLÉ CRENSHAW[1]

Superwoman or Mule?

While sitting among family and friends at a gathering, we sat with eyes glued to the television, watching the Olympic trials as athletes competed for a spot on their nation's team during the highly esteemed and anticipated 2024 Olympics in Paris, France. We all were in awe of the speed of runners, strength of swimmers, and agility of gymnasts on that day! Amongst gymnasts, a young Black woman named Simone Biles led the pack. This young, beautiful, amazing, extraordinary woman towered over many with remarkable gymnastic skills. Watching her was like seeing poetry personified. The way she could defy gravity with her flips, twists, leaps, and almost flawless landings appeared intellectually hyperbolic to the eyes—however, our eyes were not playing tricks on us. Her actions were reality!

Despite ALL of what I just described, the conversation in the room was shocking. "Sisters" (other Black women) in the room complained about how the edges of her hair looked rough. One said, "Come on, Simone, somebody needs to hand you a brush. Girl, you got to do better than that!" Another one hollered out, "Somebody please give her some gel to smooth out her edges—Girl, you look BAD!"

I could not believe my ears. I spoke up and told the complainers that Simone did not have time to worry about frizzy hair edges. She was too busy defeating competitors and winning gold medals. I also pointed out that her makeup was beautiful, her hair was in a "messy bun" (a style frequently worn by white women), and her hair actually looked kind of cute. This reasoning did not quell their arguments. They only became fiercer. One retorted, "She is trolling us! Why would she come out lookin' like that? She is just doing this as some kind of defiant act."

This back-and-forth was crazy to me. It was exactly this kind of foolishness that severely impacted Biles two years earlier. In 2021, during the Tokyo Olympics, Biles pulled out of the competition, stating that she needed a mental health break due to the *twisties*, a condition that gymnasts say creates a mental block, making them unable to keep track of their position in midair.[2] Additionally, Biles had come under an avalanche of attacks from people complaining about her physical appearance. Focused on her hair, criticisms ranged from "nappy edges," to raggedy extensions (artificial or human hair that is sown, braided, or glued onto existing hair to give the appearance of longer, thicker hair). If that were not enough, Biles was also one of over 150 women athletes who were sexually assaulted during physical exams by former sports doctor Larry Nassar.[3]

Admirably, Simone Biles has risen like a phoenix from the ashes despite all of these travesties. Wisely, Biles decided to take a mental health break, engage in mental health therapy, and do a reset. She has come back stronger than ever, winning the Laureus World Sports Award for Comeback of the Year (2024). Among numerous other honors, including being a four-time gold medal winner, Biles clinched a spot on the 2024 US Olympic Team three years in a row. She has also become a major advocate for helping people understand the importance of caring for their mental health.

I digress. Back to the family gathering discussion, I concluded my engagement with the ridiculous discussion by saying, "I'm not on this bandwagon. Simone is phenomenal. Look at all she has accomplished, yet we are focused on frizzy edges. I believe she has chosen to focus on what matters most—her mental health, her craft, and her goals. I say, GOOD FOR YOU, SIMONE!"

The phenomenon of stress and frustration that Black women experience because of conflicting and contradictory societal expectations was a driving force behind my doctoral studies. In my research, I noted how Black women often feel trapped between being characterized as the strong Black woman and carrying justified anger. Society has imposed an expectation that Black women can and should handle all the stresses of life without breaking a sweat. Black women are, as the late literary artist Zora Neale Hurston declared, "de mule uh de world."[4] This unfortunate mischaracterization of Black women has placed an unconscionable burden upon them, impacting their mental and physical well-being.[5] In my dissertation, *Lived Experiences of Inequity of African American Women Leading Struggling, Nonprofit Organizations in the United States: A Phenomenological Study*, I discuss the strong Black woman trope. This concept inculcates the racist misconception that Black people in general and Black women, in particular, are without feeling, and therefore, they are capable of handling the ugly, racist, inequitable, disenfranchising micro and macroaggressions that they receive.[6]

More than one thing can be true regarding an issue simultaneously. In this instance, the issue under consideration is the plight of women and Black and Brown people in the United States. More than ever, women have excelled in America. In every sector, women have some form of representation. Women have broken into fields that have been largely occupied by men. Women are scientists, agriculturists, mathematicians, artists, clergy, professors, physicians, morticians, construction workers, athletes, tradespersons, entrepreneurs, CEOs, etc.

One might then ask, why are we still debating, arguing, and opining over egregious inequalities experienced by women in general and women of color in particular? More broadly speaking, concerning people of color (especially Black, Indigenous, and Brown people), why are we still discussing our experiences of systemic racism, marginalization, and oppression in the United States? Are these not the questions posed by those who have been insulated from these realities?

False piety and patriarchal structures interact to create barriers to advancement opportunities for women and Black and Brown people. Somewhere, lurking beneath the painful, ugly, and unimaginable historical experiences of the oppressed, is a false notion that God, Godself, ordained it to be so. It is important to explore further layers of barriers and belief systems that undergird the perpetuation of structures that promote the aforementioned realities.

Words to Describe Experiences of Oppression, Ceilings, and Barriers

Intersectionality Theory: An ideology advanced by Kimberlé Crenshaw,[7] intersectionality theory argues that race, gender, and class intersect to create formidable systemic barriers for women of color across various sectors. Intersectionality theory emphasizes the reality that interlocking systems create barriers that seek to delegitimize the voices, experiences, and ideologies of Black women in particular.[8]

Barrier: Anything that blocks or is intended to impede passage into or through a channel. For example, gender and race can intersect to form barriers to career ascension for Black women.[9] Glass Cliff: A phenomenon describing the reality that women are more likely than men to be appointed to precarious leadership positions in unstable, dysfunctional organizations.[10]

Why Is This Ceiling Still In Place In Our Country?

A woman has yet to win enough votes in the United States Electoral College to become president. In 2016, the Democratic nominee, Secretary of State Hillary Rodham Clinton, won the popular vote, and in 2024, Vice President Kamala Harris became the second woman to win the nomination for the Democratic Convention, but they still were not elected to the highest office in our land. Patriarchy still has a stranglehold on the US despite our movement forward. As of 2025, many other nations around the world have made this leap over the fear of being led by a woman: fifty-nine, to be exact. As early as the 1960s, the following women were elected by their countries to be their highest leaders.[11] Among them are:

Sri Lanka
Sirimavo Bandaranaike, 1960

India
Indira Gandhi, 1966

Israel
Golda Meir, 1969

Argentina
Isabel Perón, 1974

Central African Republic
Elisabeth Domitien, 1975

Portugal
Maria de Lourdes Pintasilgo, 1979

United Kingdom
Margaret Thatcher, 1979

The 1990s were the top decade for expanding the list, as the most countries chose a woman to serve as their leader then. These countries included Ireland, Bangladesh, Nicaragua, Poland, Rwanda, Haiti, Canada, New Zealand, Guyana, and Switzerland. These nations are diverse, with varying levels of poverty and prosperity, varying kinds of governmental structures, and political upheavals. Yet, they were somehow able to move beyond the impediments that would keep them from entrusting their nation's top position to a woman. Complex oppressive systems developed during the founding of our nation to discriminate against Indigenous people, Black people, and women continue to haunt us to this day.

"Is She Black Enough? Is She Capable?" Is It Right? Reflections on Vice President Kamala Harris's 2019 and 2024 Presidential Bids

In the 2024 election, then–presidential candidate Donald Trump effectively used specific tactics to overcome any possibility of a Harris win. Trump again used fear, racism, and especially the fear of others (immigrants) taking away jobs from Americans, committing crimes, and poisoning the blood of our country. Trump used trans and homophobic tropes. He ran ads that convinced some people that they would send their children to school, and they would come back as the opposite sex. His campaign also ran ads with comments taken out of context, showing Harris saying that she would use tax dollars to fund sex change operations for members of the military. In fact, Harris was responding to a question about whether she would follow current US policy that allows military members to receive medical care for gender-affirming operations. Harris said that she would follow the law.

He used sexism by catering to the insecurities of some men by suggesting that women were trying to run them out of their rightful places as the leaders of their homes, as well as their nation. This ideology also spoke to some men who believe the Bible teaches male headship only. People who believe this incorrect interpretation of scripture believe it is sinful to have a woman leader over a church, a home, or a nation. All these tactics wielded great power and influence during the 2024 presidential election. With that understanding, we consider the following.

In 2019, then-senator Kamala Harris launched a bid to become the Democratic nominee for president of the United States. Previously, Senator Harris served in several other high-level positions. Prior to becoming a senator (2017–2021), Harris served as the attorney general of the State of California (2011–2017) as well as a prosecutor and district attorney. Her 2019 campaign was criticized as being weak. Some people considered her political platform to be too much like other liberals running (e.g., Senators Bernie Sanders and Elizabeth Warren), and her record as an attorney was castigated by opponents and many Black people for her tough-on-crime stance.[12]

As a California district attorney, prosecutor, and attorney general, Harris had the difficult job of prosecuting crime, enforcing policies that sought to hold all criminals accountable and reduce violence, drugs, and theft across the state. Critics complained that her policies disproportionately harmed Black people. In a high-profile case involving a Black man, she rejected the use of advanced DNA testing that could have exonerated him from death row (a decision for which she later expressed deep regret). Some constituents accused Harris of not prioritizing cases involving police killings of minorities, nor did she support a bill that would have involved the attorney general's office investigating officer-involved shootings.[13]

One has to wonder how many DAs, prosecutors, and AGs made similar calls. Were they criticized as harshly? The fact of the matter is that then-Attorney Harris was in an impossible position. The penal system disproportionately impacts Black people in general by killing, arresting, and imprisoning more Black and Brown people than is proportional to the population.[14] Clearly, she prosecuted cases that involved all ethnicities. But the spotlight was placed upon the prosecution of her own people. Had she gone easy on criminals of color, she would have been accused of being soft on crime. Harris was not the "Black attorney general" positioned to work for

Black people. She was the California attorney general, positioned to fight crime against all people.

A Black person's ethnicity is placed on trial when this kind of issue arises. Questions such as, why are they not doing more to help Black people? Why did she not do more to stop those white cops from killing Black people? Why is she acting white? Unfortunately, this is the plight of women and Black and Brown people when we step into roles traditionally withheld from us. In several of her groundbreaking roles, she was the first woman, the first Black woman, and the first woman of Southeast Asian descent. Being the first of anything can be challenging. People are more likely to criticize, demonize, demean, interrogate, and count as less than rather than honor and praise accomplishments.

In the early 2000s, Harris established a reentry program called Back on Track: A Problem-Solving Reentry Court, which was hailed as a restorative justice endeavor.[15] But this initiative did not matter to her critics. Although Harris fought to expand voting rights for individuals serving felony sentences, these efforts were ignored. Harris opposed the death penalty and maintained that stance when she refused to seek the death penalty against a gang member who was found guilty of killing a police officer. Her critics, however, did not mention that fact. Her philosophical consistency did not matter to her critics. Neither did it matter that while serving as senator, Harris praised Governor Gavin Newsom for placing a moratorium on the death penalty and that she subsequently called for a federal moratorium on executions.[16]

Harris defended California's right to use the death penalty due to her position as attorney general. Consistently, Harris also argued that in many instances, it was "immoral, discriminatory, ineffective, and a gross misuse of taxpayer dollars."[17] Harris also argued that Black and Latino defendants, as well as the poor, are disproportionately executed, in comparison to white and wealthier defendants with better legal representation.[18]

Taken together, Kamala Harris' experiences highlight the reality of many well-educated, brilliant, and gifted people of color in general and Black women in particular. We are often underestimated, overly criticized, and held to standards that are disproportionately higher than our white counterparts. Harris left her first run for the presidential nomination at the end of 2019. After dropping out of the race, she was invited by then–presidential nominee, former Vice President Joseph R. Biden to become his running mate. The Biden-Harris ticket went on to win the 2020 presidential election. Once more, Kamala Harris became the first woman, the first Black woman, and the first woman of Southeast Asian descent to serve as vice president of the United States of America. Sadly, she would not ascend to the position of national president, at least not in 2025.

Underestimated, Oppressed, and Yet Undaunted: My Parents' Lived Experiences and Possibly Many Other Women and People of Color

My Father's Story

I come from a lineage of determined people. My parents, siblings, and extended family were all born in formerly British Guyana, before gaining independence from the United Kingdom in 1966. Unfortunately, when many in America hear about Guyana, the first thing they recall is the infamous cult leader Jim Jones. Jones led hundreds of people (predominantly from America) in a mass murder-suicide in Jonestown, Guyana, in 1978. Guyana, however, was so much more. It was a diverse country in South America with several languages, brilliant people, with strength, dignity, and perseverance. Sadly, it has endured its share of economic decline and governmental upheavals over the decades. Most of my family has left, many moving to the motherland of England, Canada, or the United States of America.

In 1931, my father, Robert Alexander Small, was born in Kitty, Guyana. His father was an accountant, and his mother was a seamstress. Although my grandfather was an accomplished man, he never earned the salary that he should have as an accountant. My fraternal grandparents struggled greatly financially, but they did their best to provide for their home. By age six, my father already knew he wanted to become an American citizen.

He was a bright, ambitious, and adventurous child. With the guidance, discipline, and support of his parents, my father grew to understand that faith in Almighty God and a good education were the keys to his success. He proudly recounted that at the age of seven, his second-grade schoolmaster determined that his marks were not high enough for him to proceed to the third grade. This experience was one of the first examples of him being underestimated.

My father, even as a child, never allowed the perceptions of others to cloud his understanding of his own capabilities. Seeing the schoolmaster's decision as an unnecessary setback and a troubling hindrance to his long-term goals, he simply slipped into the third-grade classroom and worked diligently to receive high marks. By the time it was discovered that he should have been retained in the second grade, he had done so well that the schoolmaster decided to let him stay! My father never looked back but continued to excel academically and reach higher heights.

He attended St. Stanislaus College for Boys upon completion of his lower-level studies at the Georgetown School System in British Guyana, South America. Intrigued by the sciences, my father elected to study chemistry. He was underestimated once again during one of his college classes. My father had a remarkable memory. In preparation for a written exam, he memorized every aspect of a particular formula and process. He was able to write down every detail of the process and correctly apply and solve the problem given. The professor asked him to stay after class and rewrite his answer.

Without hesitation, my father did so. The professor told my father that he thought that he had somehow copied from another person or cheated. He later apologized and called him a genius.

In 1953, my father met my mother, Miss Patricia H. Garraway. They married one year later in 1954. While their life in Guyana was comfortable, father never forsook his childhood dream of becoming an American citizen. So, he decided to pursue an American degree from a historically Black college. He was accepted by both Morgan State University in Baltimore, Maryland, and Central State University in Wilberforce, Ohio. Ultimately, he chose Central State. He initially came to America alone in 1959 and struggled as an older college student at the age of twenty-eight. Father graduated from Central State with a bachelor of science degree in chemistry in 1963. His wife and children later followed him.

Before graduating, he was offered a job as a chemist with General Tire and Rubber Company in Akron, Ohio. It was the tumultuous '60s during the Civil Rights era. The challenges he experienced on the job were fierce. In addition to coming to work and finding the n-word tacked onto the bulletin board near his work area, co-workers would frequently place newspaper clippings of recent crimes committed by Black people on the board as well. Attempting to get my father fired, one of his managers deliberately provided him with inaccurate instructions to perform an important procedure. Father knew the instructions were wrong, but he chose to handle the incident strategically. Smartly, he asked the manager to write the instructions down. The foolish man did so and then threw the paper in the trash. When the man walked out of the room, my father retrieved the paper out of the trash and kept it.

A few days later, company leaders called my father into the office to explain why he made such a big mistake. When he said that his manager instructed him to do so, the man lied and said he would never give those instructions. At that point, my father pulled the paper out of his pocket and gave it to the higher-level manager. Because the man recognized the other manager's handwriting, he knew that my father was telling the truth. When asked why he would lie and do that to my father, the man replied, "I have never had to work with a negro, and it was hard for me to accept him working here as a chemist." The manager did not lose his job, although he was made to feel ashamed. The company made him apologize to my father. Several years later, another manager replaced that man. When he reviewed my father's pay history, the new manager called my father to the office to let him know that he had been severely underpaid as a chemist. To God be the glory, he increased his pay to the appropriate level, although he did not make the pay retroactive. I suspect his history of low pay was due to his skin color and not his skill level.

Both my parents were staunch Catholics. I remember as a small child putting on my "Sunday dress" (I literally had two church dresses that hung in my parents' closet) and going to church on Sunday morning. Eventually, my father stopped going to church. I did not understand why. Later, I discovered that some of my father's co-workers attended the same church as we did. When they saw my father at church, they behaved as if they did not know who he was. This hypocrisy greatly hurt and embarrassed him. After several of those encounters, he quit going, only attending church on Good Friday for the 3 p.m. service, which he would go to by himself. I do not know what he would say to the Lord, but this was seemingly his way of saying, "I'm still here Lord, I just can't deal with these people." My father's experience exemplifies common aspects of false piety. These people *attended* a gathering in a building called church, but the CHURCH was not present in the hearts of many who entered the edifice.

In 1970, my father realized his dream of becoming an American citizen. My father, mother, and three siblings (Paul, Donna, and Gillian) all became American citizens. I was born a few years prior, in 1964. As far as we know, I was the only natural-born American citizen in our family at that time, making me a first-generation American. Praise God, my father was not a sexist. He would frequently say to me, "Chrissy, do you know that you are the only one in our family who could become the president of the United States?" He encouraged all his girls to get an education and be able to take care of our own selves. He would say, "Get an education and be able to stand on your own two feet, so that if you get married and your husband decides to act like a fool, you can tell him where to go!" Later in life, when I was serving as an associate minister at a church, he would say to me, "Chrissy, don't you want your own church? Don't you want to be the pastor?" At that stage of my life, I did not want to be a pastor, but his words were indeed prophetic!

My father ended up receiving several promotions and significant accomplishments at General Tire and Rubber Company. During his time there, he led a team of chemists to develop a Reverse Addition Process, which eventually turned into a lucrative patented product for the company. I am confident that my father was not compensated as he should have been for the development of that product. After thirty years of working for the same company (New Name–GenCorp), Robert Alexander Small retired as a senior analytical chemist.

My Mother's Story

My mother, Patricia Helena Garraway, also known as "Patsy," was born in 1930 in Bartica, Guyana. Her father was a government pharmacist and community physician, and her mother was a schoolteacher. They were well-off financially and enjoyed the blessings of a large, government-supplied mansion, land, and assistance in the home. With pride and gratefulness, my mother would fondly recount the many adventures that she, her parents, sisters, cousins, and friends shared in their family home. With a natural gift for storytelling, my mother could paint a word picture of events from the past that would make anyone listening feel as if they were right there in the midst.

Momma loved sharing about her father's role as a government/community pharmacist, her father's drug store, and how he helped so many people. She said they called Daddy Garraway "Chief." He was greatly respected in the community. My mother was raised in a home of hospitality. Many guests would frequent their home and experience the kindness and compassion of her mother, Mabel, who, as a schoolteacher, would provide lunches for hungry students in her class and in the neighborhood.

Momma's home was also a home filled with music. There, visitors would experience the musical brilliance of her family, especially her sister Shirley, a concert pianist. My mother herself was a concert violinist who studied music in Guyana at the Trinity Music School and the Royal School of Music via correspondence in London, England. Her family would often hold concerts right in their home for themselves. Momma and her sister Shirley also gave community concerts in the main public hall in Georgetown. As a concert violinist, her opening and signature song was Thai's (pronounced TAZE) "Meditation." Momma was certified by the Royal Academy of Music in London, England, and was the first chair violinist in the orchestra. She received credit for piano from the Academy of Music in London.

Momma was raised in a God-fearing home. Her parents faithfully raised their family in the church. She grew to love the Lord and the work of the church. As she grew, she felt called to go into the ministry. She joined the Carmelite Order of Nuns as a Chapel Sister. There she played violin, piano, and organ for the convent. After a short period of time, however, she decided that although she loved the church and the convent, the life of a nun was not for her.

Sadly, my mother spent many years of her life grieving that she did not fulfill her calling. As a member of the Catholic Church, the only way a woman could enter the ministry was to become a nun. This extremely thick stained-glass ceiling blocked her from living out her call in the church that she loved. As a little girl, I can remember sitting on the couch with my mother in the living room, listening to her tell the story of her decision to leave the convent. Momma said that she dreamed of Mother Mary telling her that she would go back out into the world, but that she would never be happy. She then would say, "As I left the convent, I asked the Lord to call one of my children." This story became an integral part of my own call story.

Not long after leaving the convent, my mother and father met at a community party. In 1954, my parents married. Together, they were blessed with four beautiful children: my three previously mentioned siblings and eventually, me. My mother supported her husband's lifelong dream of becoming an American citizen. She did all she could to help him as he was accepted into Central State University, Wilberforce, Ohio. In 1961, my mother entrusted her three children to her mother and family and came to America. Unfortunately, her father had died of a massive cerebral hemorrhage. Although he had his will prepared, it was never signed. They lost practically everything. My grandmother, without her husband, did not have financial protection. To God be the glory, they still had one another and help from family and the community, who loved them. My grandmother continued to care for my siblings when my mother transitioned to America.

Mother traveled to New York and lived with family for a season, working menial jobs to help send financial support to her struggling husband and family back in Guyana. Having been raised in a prominent home, this was truly a labor of love and sacrifice for her family. Nevertheless, my mother worked with all her heart to ensure that her husband could finish his schooling to become a chemist, and that their children and her mother could reunite with them in America.

Momma recounted the story of working all week long, cleaning a woman's home and cooking for her family. At the end of the week, the woman handed her a five-dollar bill and asked, "What is a girl like you going to do with 'all of this money'?" Despite the horrible racism and indignities, my mother held her head high, looked at the woman, and declared, "It is not the size of the gift that matters, but the manner and heart with which it is received." She said that the woman looked at her and inquired as to where she learned how to speak in such a way. The ignorant woman did not realize that she was in the presence of a Guyanese scholar!

My parents ultimately purchased a home in Akron, Ohio, where they raised our family. In that home, my mother carried on the tradition of teaching her children about love, faith, prayer, and trust in the Lord, cooking delicious meals, hosting guests, playing beautiful music on the stereo, and sharing family stories. Sadly, she never returned to her music career, but instead, happily worked as a nursing assistant at Akron General Medical Center for approximately twenty years until her retirement. My mother worked hard and sacrificed much for her husband and her family. Though never bitter, I am confident that her mental health suffered greatly as she stifled her ministry calling, relinquished her musical career, and worked a job that was woefully unmatched to her gifts and skills. Like so many women, she laid down her life so we might live.

My parents also became sponsors for many of our relatives. As a child, I did not understand what was going on when relatives would come and stay for weeks with us. I was always excited when they came because I was thrilled to meet them and to hear all the stories about back home. Together, they would prepare delicious Guyanese cuisine—chicken, lamb, and beef curry with rice and roti, garlic pork with onions and rye bread, pepper pot with oxtail, cook-up rice made with black-eyed peas, onions, and chunks of ham, and many more amazing dishes. The house was filled with the aroma of good food, fellowship, laughter, and love!

Sometimes, however, feelings of stress and fear were palpable in the atmosphere. I heard many conversations about immigration services and concerns over deportation. It was not until later in life that I realized the pressures they faced with the challenges of the 1960s, the pain of being underestimated, undercompensated, denied equal opportunities, treated as invisible, and overwhelmed. Through it all, however, they persevered and triumphed over the ugliness of systems designed to crush them.

Barred Doors, Glass Ceilings, and Glass Cliffs—My Personal Experiences

I began keeping journals early on in life, writing down my thoughts, prayers, hopes, and dreams for my future. It never occurred to me that I would one day become an author. My writing from that time was just a way for me to process. For me, writing became a more serious endeavor when I was faced with a challenge concerning my abilities in high school. At the beginning of my tenth-grade year, students were given the opportunity to take a writing exam to determine if we were eligible to enter an AP (Advanced Placement) English class. My best friend and I decided to try it out.

The test required us to read a passage on Greek theatre. We were then tasked with describing the selection in detail, the content order, and various application forms. I was so nervous, but I gave it my best shot. The next day, we received our results. I failed, but my friend passed. The news was devastating! Undaunted, however, I went to the teacher (Ms. Bonnie Swan) and said, "Ms. Swan, I know that I did not do well on the test, but if you give me a chance, I know I can learn the material." She looked curiously at me and said she would consider my request.

As I awaited her decision, I nervously prayed for the Lord to touch her heart to give me another chance. During the preliminary classes, students were taught how to write using the five-paragraph theme approach. I worked diligently and listened intently in preparation for our next exam. When the day came, I said a prayer and wrote out my answer. The following day, I learned I had passed the exam with a B. I was relieved and overjoyed, and I felt a sense of godly pride and thankfulness that I had been given another chance and succeeded!

But then, I was confronted with the ugliness of underestimation. As I prepared to enter class one morning, Ms. Swan pulled me aside and said, "Christine, I probably should not tell you this, but I decided that I would. While in the teacher's lounge this morning, one of the teachers came to me and asked, 'What is Christine doing in your class? How did *she* end up in there?'" She never told me the name of the teacher or how she responded. Ms. Swan simply said to me, "Christine, at that moment, I made up my mind that I was going to do everything I could to help you succeed!" I shall never forget the look of determination on her face and the kindness with which she spoke to me.

Ms. Swan became my greatest advocate. I was one of a few students she invited to her beautiful home for a special time with her for dinner during the Christmas season. I can still remember the delicious chicken casserole she prepared for us, sitting in front of her large picture window, watching the snow fall, and discussing our experiences, writing, and future. God used Ms. Swan to help me to become the writer that I am today. For her, I am grateful.

I never learned what it was about me that caused the unnamed person to underestimate my abilities and skills. Their ugliness served as a reminder to me personally to get to know a person, learn who they are and what they bring to the table, and avoid callously determining that they are less than. Fast-forward, other experiences of discrimination and underestimation loomed around future corners.

I desired to pursue doctoral studies following graduation from college and seminary. My original intent was to focus on systematic theology and womanist studies. I was offered an opportunity to enter a doctor of theology program at Boston University (BU) with a full-tuition scholarship, an apartment, and an assistant teaching position. My pathway seemed clear, but then I was called by my home church pastor to return and serve as the assistant pastor. Torn between the two opportunities, I ultimately yielded to the pull of God's Holy Spirit and turned down the offer from BU. While I never doubted that I made the right decision, I struggled with anger and resentment, not understanding at the time that the Lord was preparing me for great blessings along the path of obedience.

Upon returning home, I was not given the position promised. I was not ordained as promised. An unfortunate firestorm of painful events ensued. Unbeknownst to us, our pastor was having a nervous breakdown. Although I have no official proof of this, he had apparently been suffering from some form of mental illness that had been well-controlled for many years. Possibly the pressures of the ministry broke him. He began to falsely accuse members of many ungodly things.

He accused me of having an affair with a married man and told me that if I did not confess and repent, I would be put out of the church and stripped of my ministerial license. No words could possibly explain the confusion, pain, and embarrassment that I experienced. Long story short, I did not confess to something that was not true. As a result, I was put out of the church and excommunicated. They nullified the license that I received to preach at age seventeen. Members were forbidden to speak to me. I became a literal outcast to people I had known and loved since my teenage years. But God had a plan.

I began attending church for about six months with an apostolic congregation. My mother, with great support and love, came with me. Our journey there was a time of healing, rebuilding, and restoring. Ultimately, we ended up joining another church in Cleveland, Ohio. This church was familiar to us, as our former pastor was a son of the church, and we attended there many times during conferences, Christian education institutes, and revivals. The senior pastor was familiar with the unfortunate turn of events and kindly accepted me under his wing. After a time of prayerful observation, he relicensed me and subsequently ordained me a few years later. In that place, God sent me my husband. We were blessed with three beautiful children and the ministry work the Lord had prepared for my journey began.

Keepers of the Keys: Tactics Used to Bar Entrance to Certain Fields of Study

Predominantly white institutions (PWIs) of higher learning historically maintain barriers to entrance to certain fields by minorities. Frequently, they use standardized tests and committees stacked with racially biased interviewers. They often redirect individuals to what they perceive as more appropriate fields of study. After working at the church as minister of Christian education for three years, I felt drawn again to pursue doctoral studies. I began working as a part-time research assistant in the department of psychology at Case Western Reserve University. I have always felt an affinity for psychological studies and desired to become a psychologist. It was a blessing to work as an assistant to a godly, sensitive, and brilliant professor in the psychology department. I shared my dreams and goal of becoming a psychologist with her, and together, we began to work through a plan to possibly get me accepted into a program at the school. After a year of serving in the department, I applied to be accepted into the PhD program. On a positive note, my application was reviewed and advanced to the interview stage.

My interview was scheduled with the head of the department. During the process, he questioned me about why I wanted or needed a PhD. Initially, I did not see this as particularly unusual until he began to press the issue. To my utter dismay, the persistent tone and tenor of his questioning felt dismissive and demeaning. He said, "I don't see why you need a PhD. Can't you help people doing what you already do as a pastor? Don't you want to get paid? The people you will probably serve won't be able to pay you!" I was shocked by his line of reasoning. After further comments, he clearly believed that I would only be able to serve poor, Black people. I responded by letting him know that I believed that I would serve all kinds of people regardless of race or financial capabilities. He was not impressed.

The professor I assisted later shared that the decision-making team was evenly split concerning my acceptance. The department chair cast the tie-breaking vote against my acceptance. I was devastated. I continued working as a research assistant and applied again the next year. I was rejected once more. After that, I left the position and did not return to the school. In the early 2000s, the Case department of psychology only accepted a small percentage of Black students. I was told that most of the Black students applied and were accepted to the department of social work. Those in decision-making positions apparently believed that social work was more suited to Black people.

Black people continue to make up a minuscule percentage of psychologists in America. As reported by the Association of Black Psychologists, approximately 4 percent of psychologists, 22 percent of social workers, 7 percent of marriage and family counselors, and 11 percent of professional counselors are Black. According to the Government Accountability Office (GAO), there were approximately 1.2 million behavioral health providers in the US in 2020.[19]

In recent years, organizations like the American Psychological Association have sought to remedy this blatantly racist barrier that keeps Black people from entering the profession. Mental health care professionals are beginning to acknowledge that these barriers cannot persist. They are directly addressing barriers by offering intentional internships, extending calls for scholarly, peer-reviewed articles, and mentoring programs for minorities in general and Black people in particular. There is an increased recognition that people of color bring critical perspectives, diversity, and value to the field. Too often, minorities are the *subjects* of studies, rather than the *writers* of their lived experiences in academia and behavioral health practices. This underrepresentation of minorities in fields like psychology correlates strongly with racist, historical perceptions that Black people are genetically inferior, have smaller brains, and are intellectually incapable of higher levels of reasoning.

Following the COVID-19 pandemic, some colleges and universities stopped using standardized testing altogether or reduced the level of significance they play in determining the capabilities and potential of students. Standardized tests disproportionately impact certain minority groups through cultural bias. Success on these tests largely depends upon a student's upbringing, the schools they attended, the geographical area of their home, etc. Students from less privileged backgrounds may not have been exposed to any number of academic opportunities. Wealthier students of all races have the resources to pay for and take SAT and ACT test classes. Frequently, they take the test two to three times before actually sitting for the test prior to college. These classes can cost upward of $1,000 or more. These opportunities unfairly advantage them to achieve higher scores.[20]

At the University of California, Los Angeles (UCLA), the Civil Rights Project found substantial test-score differences between ethnic and socioeconomic groups. Studies show that, on average, Asian and white students score higher than Black, Hispanic, and Native American students. Generally speaking, students from higher-income families score significantly better than students from lower-income families. These observations have led many colleges and universities to focus less on test scores and more on high school performance in terms of grades and personal character to increase equity and parity. Doing so also increases much-desired diversity across cultures and socioeconomic status.[21]

Scapegoats, Trickery, and Greed

Taken together, one can reasonably assert that specific minority groups can be pigeonholed—or rigidly assigned to a role based on assumptions—not because of capability, but because of a lack of exposure to greater academic opportunities, finances, and the effects of classism and racism. Many who have been excluded or passed over due to pigeonholing are filled with potential, are brilliant, and are extraordinarily capable. Unfortunately, in 2025, the Trump administration made abundantly clear that all things DEI (Diversity, Equity, and Inclusion) would be rolled back. President Trump made good on his threats to pull federal funds from any colleges or universities that support DEI initiatives on his first day in office. He signed executive orders closing all DEI government offices and placing all government employees working within those offices on leave, eventually being laid off. In a gangster move, the Trump administration warned federal employees that all who did not report coworkers who tried to manipulate wording or alter job descriptions to cover up DEI initiatives would experience "adverse consequences."[22]

Increasing numbers of businesses have also been removing DEI language from their policies. According to *Inc.*, Ford, Boeing, Caterpillar, Harley-Davidson, Black & Decker, John Deere, and rural retailer Tractor Supply are now on that list.[23] Target, Walmart, and McDonald's have joined them.

Americans were convinced that an immigrant invasion of sorts was the reason why the working class was suffering. Much of the general public and the politicians who represent them scapegoated Brown people in particular as the reason behind a perceived scarcity of goods and services, jobs, and opportunities in our nation. Tragically, the politicians' trickery worked. Many political pundits declared that the Democrats lost the 2024 election because they abandoned the working class and no longer understood how to speak their language. In an interesting twist, several of the same people who championed the deportation millions of immigrants to "make America great again" began pushing policies to bring in highly trained foreigners, pay them less, and hire them in place of American citizens.

Elon Musk and Vivek Ramaswamy, billionaires tapped by President Trump to lead the Department of Government Efficiency (DOGE—a newly formed ad hoc committee with no congressional oversight or accountability) began to encourage Trump to increase the number of foreign tech workers. In 2020, Trump's administration limited the number of H-1B visas that enabled foreign engineers and skilled workers from other nations to come to the country to work for big tech companies.[24] Notably, both Musk and Ramaswamy use these workers to advance their own business interests. By doing so, they did exactly what they claimed would harm the American working class. They did a bait and switch. They sold Americans a false bill of goods. They were masterful in their use of fear and hatred of foreigners, despite the fact that Musk himself is a native South African and Ramaswamy gained US citizenship through birth (both of his parents were non-citizens at the time). These men have profited significantly on the backs of struggling, unsuspecting voters.

On January 7, 2025, days before being sworn into office for the second time, Trump held a press conference where he heralded his perceived negotiation skills. He celebrated his threats to pull military and economic support from NATO (The North Atlantic Treaty Organization—an organization created to protect the freedom and security of its members through political, military, and economic support) if other members did not pay what he considered to be their fair share. He justified his position by claiming that other nations are behind in the required 2 percent of their GDP (Gross Domestic Product) contributions to the collaborative pot of monies to support all members. According to the 2024 NATO Expense Report, the US pays approximately 3.38 percent of its GDP. The only nation that has reported a higher percentage is Poland at 4.12 percent. The majority of the other nations came in above 2.0 percent, with only a few below that marker.[25]

At first glance, Trump's bluster may appear justified. Why should the US bring more to the table? What was not explained was that our country holds military interests in other parts of the world outside of NATO, giving the impression that our contributions are significantly higher than those of others. The fact of the matter is that our contributions are proportionate to our wealth, and the wealth (or lack thereof) of the other countries. As of 2024, the US maintains the highest and strongest GDP/economy in the world, coming in at a whopping $29.17 trillion.[26] Why does this matter?

Politicians speak a language that is foreign to the majority of listeners. They often paint a picture that is bleak when they are not in office, while hiding important truths, such as no president can control the cost of eggs. Because we live in a capitalist society, the free market controls the price of goods, products, wares, etc. Global markets are impacted by natural events such as poor crops, pandemics, wildfires, hurricanes, and floods.

Governmental leaders can wisely manage *how* their country assists their citizens in terms of coping with economic fallouts. For example, several countries provided COVID-19 relief funds to businesses and workers so that they could handle the loss of revenue during lockdowns. Although the Biden administration was disparaged for monies used for the above-named purposes, many a life was saved and a business buoyed because they received assistance. Not only that, but the US also recovered economically more swiftly than other countries and emerged unpredictably strong because of the way the pandemic was managed.

Unfortunately, a strong economy does not automatically translate to the economic well-being of the proverbial kitchen table. Sadly, big businesses and corporations took advantage of the struggles and fears of the citizenry by hiking up the prices of groceries, gas, household items, and prescription drugs. As a result, people blamed the national leader, and they were encouraged to do so by those who benefited from their lack of knowledge. Price gouging is a real thing.

Trump persuaded voters to think his administration would bring prices down, create more jobs for the American worker, and push out immigrants. Instead, the nation is facing a return to environmental travesties that will increase global warming, like deregulating oil drilling, increasing carbon emissions, and dumping pollution into our water and air. They have broken relationships with our international allies through threats of massive tariffs, which are taxes on foreign goods that in turn increase the prices of products here, and threats to use military force to invade and overtake other countries. Trump has openly suggested a willingness to use the military to take back the Panama Canal, to take over Greenland, and to annex Canada. Indeed, these tactics are reminiscent of MLK's words regarding the three evils of society—racism, greed, and excessive militarism.

Landing on the Cliff: Why Black and Brown Women are Hired to Lead Broken Organizations

In *Beyond the Stained Glass Ceiling,* I unpack the reality that women pastors in general and Black women pastors in particular are frequently called to serve "Lazarus churches."[27] In the Gospel of John, the brother of Mary and Martha, Lazarus, has died. Although they sent word to Jesus that Lazarus was sick, Jesus waited until Lazarus had been dead for four days before showing up. Upon Jesus' arrival, both Mary and Martha were grieved and perplexed that he waited so long before coming. Jesus, however, knew that greater was on the way. Lazarus would be resurrected (John 11:1-44).

The Lazarus churches are ones in which, long after the male pastors have left the church, the money has dried up, and the infrastructure is completely broken, they call a woman to serve as lead pastor in a last-ditch effort for life anew. This truth is not a reflection upon women. Rather, it is the unfortunate reality that sexism based upon bad theology is alive and well, sadly, in the church. The gender wage gap might also play a role in this, as women clergy are generally paid less than their male counterparts.[28] Even amid such painful and dire situations, Jesus can still show up and bring about a resurrection (I speak from experience). The journey, however, can be wearying, daunting, and self-esteem pummeling. It is one thing for a minister to believe they have been called to serve a severely diminished church. It is a different story to be relegated to such circumstances.

Often, women find themselves stifled in both sacred and secular realms. We experience what I have termed "complexities of the imago Dei" (Latin for Image of God). In the first creation story, women and men are made in the image of God and have been given equal dominion over the earth (Genesis 1:27-28). This version of the creation of men and women is frequently ignored in favor of the second creation story found in Genesis 2 and 3, where we see the Garden of Eden story. In the garden, both Adam and Eve have dominion over every beast of the field and air, every form of vegetation, and greenery. God also commanded Adam not to eat from the tree of the knowledge of good and evil, for on the day he did so, he would die (Genesis 2:1-17). By extension, Eve was warned of the same. Unfortunately, Eve engaged in a conversation with the serpent and was tricked into eating fruit from the tree, and gave some of the fruit to Adam.

The Genesis 2 text has been misused to blame women for the fall of humanity. For those who believe in oppressing women, this passage serves as a primary go-to scripture for explaining why women should not be given head or leadership positions. Women—gifted, called, anointed, well-prepared—are made in the image of God and given equal dominion, yet are denied the authority thereof. To this day, major denominations hold to this bad theology.

In June 2024, the Southern Baptist Convention (SBC) called together their church delegates to inculcate into their constitution the repudiation and excommunication of churches that allowed women to serve in any pastoral positions. They based their suppositions upon a flawed belief that the Bible does not allow women to serve as pastors. Their attempts, however, fell short of the two-thirds majority necessary to pass the amendment.[29] The problem was that a growing number of churches within the SBC, particularly in Black and Brown congregations, have women serving in key pastoral roles. With major investments in luring minority churches into the SBC, much was at stake by kicking these churches out of the fellowship.

While many of those same congregations believe that women need to be covered by male leadership (in other words, they still need to have a male leader in authority over them), they nonetheless allow for women to lead certain ministries within the church and hold the title of pastor.[30] Opponents argued the amendment was unnecessary because their constitution already clearly states that churches calling women to serve as pastors are subject to expulsion. Churches with women in pastoral roles also argued that Baptists are autonomous and therefore have the sole authority to determine the makeup of the pastoral staff.[31] Seemingly, the loss of financial investments and future income, rather than concerns about equality for women, aborted their draconian agenda.

Glass Cliffs in Religious and Secular Organizations

In the secular realm, like the religious sector, women are frequently called to lead organizations that are economically depressed, have broken infrastructures, and near death. This is known as the glass cliff. The glass cliff phenomenon describes the reality that women are more likely than men to be appointed to precarious leadership positions in unstable, dysfunctional organizations.[32] For example, a woman may finally be hired as the CEO of a nonprofit organization, but the organization is in financial peril and on the brink of bankruptcy. Fledgling organizations frequently look to women CEOs during turbulent times, as men often reject the position. It also can mean that while the organization itself may be financially solvent, the conditions under which a woman finds herself working may be untenable due to inequitable treatment. These conditions are especially true for Black women nonprofit leaders who are most frequently hired to lead struggling organizations across nonprofit sectors.

Frequently, the social ties and networks that Black people in general and Black women in particular work within place them at a disadvantage as they endeavor to navigate organizational contexts. Societal impositions of low expectations due to family histories, consistently lower wages, and fewer opportunities to climb corporate ladders relegate them to positions with below-standard pay. Limited exposure to professional networks, organizational mentors, and opportunities to obtain appropriate salaries commensurate with their qualifications combine to impede Black job seekers' salary ascension.[33] When a Black woman does receive a promotion, research shows that she is frequently hired to lead when the organization is at its worst.[34] The standards by which Black women leaders are judged are commonly inequitable.

Scholars Courtney L. McCluney, Lauren L. Schmitz, Margaret T. Hicken, and Amanda Sonnega state that women in general and Black women in particular disproportionately experience unfair criticisms regarding their leadership.[35] Professors Jacqueline McDowell and Akilah Carter-Francique suggest further that Black women leaders are often charged with turning failing organizations around with minimal resources to do so.[36] When the organization fails to rise, remains financially unstable, or is unable to draw new talent, the blame is placed at the Black woman's feet. She is labeled a failure. These factors are examples of the inequalities experienced by Black women leaders.

Fortune.com states that in 2024, approximately 10 percent of Fortune 500 businesses were headed by women.[37] However, less than one percent of those women are non-white according to POCIT (People of Color in Tech).[38] The glass cliff phenomenon can also be related to leading organizations where resentment, stereotypical attitudes, sexism, and racism engulf a woman leader. Research suggests that women attaining leadership status in some larger organizations would leave their higher-level appointments due to a lack of organizational support, frustration, and disillusionment. The glass cliff represents more than just working in financially unstable organizations. Management and leadership scholars Seung-Hwan Jeong, Ann Mooney Murphy, and Yangyang Zhang share that investors habitually exhibit negative reactions to the appointment of Black individuals to top management positions.[39] Negativity may be manifested by the withdrawal of investments from the organization, an increase in criticisms on the handling of financial portfolios, or microaggressions in the form of derogatory comments, decreased personal involvement, or fewer referrals. As a result, minority leaders may be pushed off the glass cliff and fired in the best interest of the organization.

The findings suggest that women, specifically Black women, working within these organizations are at risk of developing mental health issues such as depression, anxiety, and stress due to the inequities and gender-related aggressions they experience. These findings remain consistent with current-day research exploring the effects of inequitable and racially hostile work environments on the health of Black women.[40]

For sure, the reality of the glass cliff poses many risks and health hazards for women. As discussions around diversity, equity, and inclusion are endangered, those invested in DEI must continue the work of creating systemic support for firsts, especially women of color. Organizations must implement well-thought-out strategies alongside appointments and succession plans for women leaders. Cultural competency courses, workshops, and training sessions must include more than an hour-long discussion and a video. Organizations seeking to embrace women leaders should invest time and money in nurturing cultural appreciation, respect, and education to dismantle the effects of stereotypes and ignorance.

Kimberlé Crenshaw nailed it when she introduced intersectionality theory. Indeed, race, gender, and class intersect to create formidable systemic barriers for women of color across a variety of sectors. Many continue to experience interlocking systems that delegitimize the voices, experiences, and ideologies, particularly Black women. Glass cliffs also remain an issue. Women continue to be more likely than men to be appointed to precarious leadership positions in unstable, dysfunctional organizations. The interplay between false piety, patriarchal structures, and barriers to advancement opportunities for women, Black and Brown people, remains a struggle. The false notion that God ordained this systemic oppression remains a part of our historic American experience. If we are to move forward as a nation, we must first acknowledge our historic roots of colonialism, false piety, violence, and oppression of specific groups of people. Only then will we be able to go about the business of genuinely creating a more perfect union.

Questions and Discussion Starters

Below are questions to help you contemplate, process, and share your thoughts.

1. In what ways have the intersections of race, gender, and class influenced how we relate to one another?
2. In your own words, explain the importance of recognizing that we all are made in the image of God.
3. How has false piety influenced modern-day politics in America?

4. Has your organization or church addressed racism, classism, and or gender discrimination? If so, how?
5. List one thing that you can do (in addition to praying) to help someone experiencing racism, classism, or gender discrimination in your community, organization, church, etc.

NOTES

1. Katy Steinmetz, "She Coined the Term 'Intersectionality' Over 30 Years Ago. Here's What It Means to Her Today," *Time,* February 20, 2020, https://time.com/5786710/kimberle-crenshaw-intersectionality/.

2. Madeline Holcombe, "What we can learn from Simone Biles' mental health break," *CNN,* Wednesday, August 9, 2023, https://www.cnn.com/2023/08/09/health/biles-mental-health-break-wellness/index.html#:~:text=In%20the%20time%20since%20she,the%20prioritization%20of%20mental%20health.

3. Ed White, "Simone Biles, other women seek $1B-plus from FBI over Nassar," *Associated Press,* June 8, 2022, https://apnews.com/article/simone-biles-sports-larry-nassar-5aee7d6f66009dcae571249481a3558f.

4. Zora Neale Hurston, *Their Eyes Were Watching God* (J.B. Lippincott, 1937).

5. Lisa F. Platt and Sandy C. Fanning, "The strong Black woman concept: Associated demographic characteristics and perceived stress among Black women," *Journal of Black Psychology,* 49 No. 1, (2022): 58–84, https://doi.org/10.1177/00957984221096211.

6. Christine A. Smith, "Lived Experiences of Inequity of African American Women Leading Struggling, Nonprofit Organizations in the United States: A Phenomenological Study" (Dissertation, Capella University, 2022), ProQuest Dissertations Publishing, 28964693, 34.

7. Kimberlé Crenshaw, "Demarginalizing the Intersection of Race and Sex: A Black Feminist Critique of Antidiscrimination Doctrine, Feminist Theory and Antiracist Politics," *University of Chicago Legal Forum,* 1 no. 8 (1989): 139–67.

8. Smith, "Lived Experiences of Inequity of African American Women Leading Struggling, Nonprofit Organizations in the United States," 112.

9. Erica D. Gamble and Norma J. Turner, "Career ascension of African American women in executive positions in postsecondary institutions," *Journal of Organizational Culture, Communications and Conflict* 19, no. 1 (2015): 82.

10. Michelle K. Ryan, S. Alexander Haslam, Thekla Morgenroth, Rink Floor, Janka Stoker, and Kim Peter, "Getting on top of the glass cliff: Reviewing a decade of evidence, explanations, and impact." *The Leadership Quarterly* 27, no. 3 (2016): 446–55.

11. Amanda Wills, Jacque Smith, and Casey Hicks, "All the countries that had a woman leader before the US," *CNN*, January 28, 2019, https://www.cnn.com/interactive/2016/06/politics/women-world-leaders/.

12. Tracy Grant and Gregory L. McNamee, "Kamala Harris." *Encyclopedia Britannica*, September 2, 2024, https://www.britannica.com/biography/Kamala-Harris.

13. Grant and McNamee, "Kamala Harris."

14. Michelle Alexander, 2010. *The New Jim Crow: Mass Incarceration in the Age of Colorblindness*. Chicago: Samuel Dewitt Proctor Conference, Inc.

15. Jacquelyn L. Rivers and Lenore Anderson, "Back on Track: A Problem-Solving Reentry Court," *BJA Fact Sheet*, September 2009, https://bja.ojp.gov/sites/g/files/xyckuh186/files/Publications/BackonTrackFS.pdf.

16. CBS News Bay Area, "Harris Calls For Federal Moratorium on Executions in Wake of Newsom's Order," *CBS News Bay Area*, March 15, 2019, https://www.cbsnews.com/sanfrancisco/news/kamala-harris-federal-moratorium-executions/.

17. CBS News Bay Area, "Harris Calls For Federal Moratorium on Executions in Wake of Newsom's Order."

18. CBS News Bay Area, "Harris Calls For Federal Moratorium on Executions in Wake of Newsom's Order."

19. Black Mental Health Workforce, (n.d.) https://abpsi.org/blackmhworkforce/#:~:text=Nationally%2C%204%25%20of%20psychologists%20(,are%20reported%20to%20be%20Black.

20. "SAT Test Prep | Improve Your SAT Score | The Princeton Review." 2016. Princetonreview.com. 2016. https://www.princetonreview.com/college/sat-test-prep.

21. Rebecca Zwick and Patricia Gándara (Foreword), "The Role of Standardized Tests in College Admissions," *UCLA The Civil Rights Project*, June 8, 2023, https://civilrightsproject.ucla.edu/news/research/college-access/admissions/the-role-of-standardized-tests-in-college-admissions.

22. Erik De La Garza, "Adverse Consequences': Trump threatens federal workers for failing to report DEI programs," *Newsbreak*, January 23, 2025, https://www.newsbreak.com/raw-story-2096750/3773257494518-adverse-consequences-trump-threatens-federal-workers-for-failing-to-report-dei-programs.

23. Bruce Crumley, "Walmart Joins Growing List of Companies Dropping DEI Policies," *Inc.*, November 26, 2024, https://www.inc.com/bruce-crumley/walmart-joins-growing-list-of-companies-dropping-dei-policies/91024542.

24. Aimee Picchi, "Musk and Ramaswamy are sparking a debate over the H-1B visa. Here's what to know about the visa," *CBS News*, December 30, 2024, https://www.cbsnews.com/news/musk-vivek-ramaswamy-h1b-visa-maga-immigration-what-to-know/.

25. Nato Expense Report, "Defense Expenditure of NATO Countries (2014-2024)," *Nato Expense Report*, 2024, 9, https://www.nato.int/nato_static_fl2014/assets/pdf/2024/6/pdf/240617-def-exp-2024-en.pdf.

26. Forbes India, 2024 January 10, "The top 10 largest economies in the world in 2025," *forbesindia.com,* https://www.forbesindia.com/article/explainers/top-10-largest-economies-in-the-world/86159/1#:~:text=The%20United%20States%20of%20America&text=The%20United%20States%20upholds%20its,and%20experiences%20advantageous%20business%20conditions.

27. Christine A. Smith, *Beyond the Stained Glass Ceiling: Equipping & Encouraging Female Pastors* (Judson Press, 2013), 26–27.

28. Kristin Knudsen, "Women, Clergypersons of Color Earn Less: Less Seniority, Lower-paying Pulpits Lend to Pay Gaps," ResourceUMC, November 2011, https://www.resourceumc.org/en/partners/gcsrw/home/content/women-clergypersons-of-color-earn-less.

29. "Southern Baptists Narrowly Reject Formal Ban on Churches with Any Women Pastors." *AP News*, June 12, 2024, https://apnews.com/article/southern-baptist-churches-women-pastors-34edfd1578e-609c3acb187ab90f0255e.

30. Bob Smietana, "Black Churches Concerned About Expulsion From SBC," *Christianity Today*, July 10, 2023, https://www.christianitytoday.com/news/2023/july/black-churches-concerned-about-expulsion-from-southern-bapt.html.

31. Smietana, "Black Churches Concerned About Expulsion from SBC."

32. Maral Darouei and Helen Pluut, "The paradox of being on the glass cliff: Why do women accept risky leadership positions?" *Career Development International,* 23 no. 4, (2018): 397–426, https://doi.org/10.1108/CDI-01-2018-0024.

33. Christine A. Smith, 2022, 39, *Lived Experiences of Inequity of African American Women Leading Struggling, Nonprofit Organizations in the United States: A Phenomenological Study*, Capella University, ProQuest Dissertations Publishing, 28964693.

34. Christine A. Smith, 39.

35. Courtney L. McCluney, Lauren L. Schmitz, Margaret T. Hicken, and Amanda Sonnega, "Structural racism in the workplace: Does perception matter for health inequalities?" S*ocial Science & Medicine*, February 2018, 199, 106–114, https://doi.org/10.1016/j.socscimed.2017.05.039.

36. Jacqueline McDowell and Akilah Carter-Francique, "An Intersectional Analysis of the Workplace Experiences of African American Female Athletic Directors," *Sex Roles,* 77 no. 5, (2017): 393–408, https://doi.org/10.1007/S11199-016-0730-Y.

37. Emma Hinchliffe and Joey Abrams, "The share of Fortune 500 businesses run by women can't seem to budge beyond 10%," *Fortune,* June 4, 2024, https://fortune.com/2024/06/04/share-of-fortune-500-businesses-run-by-women/.

38. Kumba Kpakima, "More Women Are Becoming Fortune 500 CEO's, But Only Three of Them Are WOC," *POCIT,* January 27, 2023,

https://peopleofcolorintech.com/articles/more-women-are-becoming-fortune-500-ceos-but-only-three-of-them-are-woc/.

39. Seung-Hwan Jeong, Ann Mooney Murphy, and Yangyang Zhang, "Investor Reactions to Minority CEO Appointments: The Intersection of Race-Ethnicity and Gender," *Academy of Management,* July 26, 2021, https://journals.aom.org/doi/10.5465/AMBPP.2021.266.

40. Torsheika Maddox, "Professional Women's Well-Being: The Role of Discrimination and Occupational Characteristics." *Women & Health* 53, no. 7, (2013), 706–29, https://doi.org/10.1080/03630242.2013.822455.

CHAPTER 4

What We Know, What We Have Yet to Discover

Learn to do good.
Seek justice,
Rebuke the ruthless,
Defend the fatherless,
Plead for the [rights of the] widow [in court].
—*Isaiah 1:17, AMP*

The master's tools will never dismantle the master's house.[1]
—AUDRE LORDE

What We Know About False Piety, Nationalism, and the Erasure of History

Some political leaders and candidates continue their insidious attempt to link godliness, patriotism, and historical amnesia together. The perpetrators of this false ideology peddle deceitful propaganda, suggesting people whose ancestors were enslaved and systemically oppressed by America should forgive and forget what was done. They use statements like, "That happened centuries ago, none of us were even alive during those times, we should not use what happened in the past to explain why we are not doing better in our lives," etc., to justify whitewashing history.

Indeed, God's people are called upon to forgive our enemies and those who have intentionally or unintentionally harmed us. Nowhere is it written, however, that we are required to forget our history. Forgive and forget are not synonyms. The Bible itself recounts all the stories of the good, the bad, and the ugly to instruct, advise, and forewarn humankind against wicked and foolish ways. In no way does this suggest that we should keep a list of things people have done to us in our proverbial coat jacket. To do so would be to harm our own growth, healing, and development. It does mean that we should remain aware of historical factors that shape our realities and impact our progress or lack thereof.

In *The Princeton Summer Journal,* Eunice Choi discusses "America's history of erasing history."[2] Referencing a 2017 Southern Poverty Law Center study, Choi outlines the low percentage of high school seniors surveyed (8 percent) who realized that slavery was the main driver of the Civil War. Additionally, approximately 40 percent of teachers surveyed believed states did not provide the necessary educational tools to support American history instruction concerning slavery. An even larger number of those teachers (58 percent) believed that the textbooks they were given for the instruction lacked historical integrity on the matter.[3]

In 2022-2023, the state of Florida became a leading force in banning books from schools and libraries. The Florida legislature, prompted by powerful lobbyists from the religious right and signed into law by Governor Ron DeSantis, began the removal of books from schools and public libraries. Many of the banned books provided historical facts concerning slavery in America (a topic deemed non-patriotic and disparaging of our nation). Some banned included novels/fiction that portrayed real-life experiences of certain eras and relatable stories within historical contexts. Also, they banned works that were sexually explicit, filled with sexual innuendo, and anything they perceived to be inappropriate for children (including LGBTQ+ content).[4]

To be clear, parents should have the right to object to materials they feel would be harmful or inappropriate for their children (explicit sexual content, in particular). Many schools already have remedies for such objections (letters sent home to parents informing them of materials to be read and permission for their children to participate in these lessons). With exception, however, should be history books that teach students about the truths of how America was established. Students should not be sheltered from history because it might make them feel bad or uncomfortable. The heinous practice of slavery, for example, the stealing of lands and the horrific treatment of Indigenous people, or the internment of Japanese Americans during World War II, etc., *should* make all of us uncomfortable. To impose mandates, restrictions, and forced removal of history books and classic literature from schools and libraries infringes upon family and individual rights.

I remember reading many of these books when I was a student in public school. The books were eye-opening, sometimes haunting, and often inspiring. As students, reading these books helped to broaden our perspectives on life, exposed us to both tragedy and triumph, and taught us a variety of literary forms. How unfortunate that students living in states governed by hypocrisy, overreach, and concern for political gains, rather than the education of children, will miss out on classic literary works!

Below are examples of books that have been banned:

Gone With the Wind, Margaret Mitchell
Animal Farm, George Orwell
Of Mice and Men, John Steinbeck
To Kill a Mockingbird, Harper Lee
The Color Purple, Alice Walker
Native Son, Richard Wright
Go Tell It On the Mountain, James Baldwin
For Whom the Bell Tolls, Ernest Hemingway
The Great Gatsby, F. Scott Fitzgerald
The Lord of the Flies, William Golding
I Know Why the Caged Bird Sings, Maya Angelou

Their Eyes Were Watching God, Zora Neale Hurston
Invisible Man, Ralph Ellison[5]

According to the American Library Association, Florida had the most books banned or attempted book bans in the United States. Approximately 2,700 books were targeted for removal or restrictions in Florida schools and public libraries.[6] Florida even surpassed Texas in this regard. Freedom in America is for all Americans, not just those with certain opinions. Individuals and parents who understand this truth vehemently fought back against Governor Ron DeSantis and the Florida lawmakers. Challenges to these rulings continue to expand.

The erasure of history is not new. As a means to forcibly change the enslaved person's self-perception, yield to the slaver's ownership, and disorient them from anything that might empower them, such as culture, worth, family, etc., they acted to beat their history out of them. This brutal and inconceivably evil practice was depicted in the 1970s series *Roots.*[7]

Historian and autobiographer Alex Haley's riveting made-for-television series *Roots* told the story of his proud, culturally rich ancestral African lineage from Gambia and their tragic enslavement during the infamous Transatlantic slave trade. In one of the more famous scenes, Haley's ancestor, a young, strong, brilliant, skilled Mandinka warrior named Kunta Kinte, along with hundreds more, was captured by European slave traders and brought to America. As part of the breaking-in process, the slaves were stripped of their language, separated from anyone (family, tribe, community) who spoke their language, and renamed. They were whipped until they called themselves by their new enslaved name.

Proud and ever resilient, Kunta boldly refused to call himself "Toby." The slaver yelled, "What is your name?" "Kunta Kinte!" The whip continued to slash against his back with the same question, "What is your name?" "Kunta Kinte!" After being whipped within an inch of his life, back ripped open, bleeding, and sun-scorched, he finally relents vocally, but inwardly, he never gave up on his dream of one day returning to his homeland. Unfortunately, that dream was never realized. Centuries later, Kunta's story, told by his ancestor, forced many to catch a glimpse of America's roots.[8]

Alex Haley's biography powerfully depicts his ancestry in a way that would not likely have been shared through another mind's eye. Movies such as *Gone with the Wind* (1940) glorified the Antebellum South. Slaves were portrayed as happy, "simple-minded darkies" who adored their slave owners and would give their lives for them against the dirty, evil Yankees who came to ruin their picturesque existence. Movies such as *The Birth of a Nation* (1915) celebrated the Ku Klux Klan as protectors of the realm, so to speak (especially white women), who rescued their communities from being brought under subjection to cruel, undignified, lust-filled Mulattos, as well as dark-skinned, big lipped, bucking eyes rapists, robbers, and the like.[9]

Very few Black film directors have been able to break into the broader film production industry. The first Black man credited with being a filmmaker was Oscar Micheaux.[10] Although he was born into slavery, following his emancipation, he worked as a Pullman porter. Later, however, he followed his dream of becoming a writer and subsequently a filmmaker. In 1919, he made history when he became the first Black person to produce a feature-length film, *The Homesteader*, based on his self-published novel.[11]

He paved the way for Black filmmakers, television series, screenwriters, and directors, who would follow in his footsteps over one hundred years later. Spike Lee, Tyler Perry, Lee Daniels, Nicole Hannah Jones, and Shonda Rhimes are just some of those who have taken up the mantle to tell stories of the lived experiences of Black people during slavery, the Civil Rights era, and current times. Their manner of storytelling was not always sorrowful and tragic. Their creativity encompasses a variety of artistic genres, including history, comedy, romance, sitcoms, documentaries, and horror.

Movies, series, and documentaries such as *Do the Right Thing, Malcolm X, The Butler, Madea* franchise (in 2015, billionaire Tyler Perry purchased a former Confederate Army base, Fort McPherson in Atlanta, Georgia, repurposing it as his massive motion picture studio, "Tyler Perry Studios")[12], *Queen Charlotte* (part of the *Bridgerton* Series), *Grey's Anatomy, The 1619 Project,* and Tyler Perry's 2024 production *Six Triple Eight* (focused upon the first and only Women's Army Corps unit of color to serve overseas in WWII) are examples of the power, importance, enlightenment, and insights offered to the world when Black voices have the opportunity to tell the story rather than always yielding to someone else's version of our reality.

The Importance of Black and Brown Voices in the Academy

Increasing the number of intellectual voices of Black and Latina women scholars in academia is critical for the training and preparation of current and future generations. Current Black and Latina women scholars and students in traditionally European American colleges and universities continue to raise concerns regarding the absence or sanitization of intersectionality theory in mainstream literature.[13] The ideologies related to gender and racial inequalities are often watered down to make messages more palatable for fear of the loss of revenue and *white fragility*.[14] White fragility is the concept that it is difficult, offensive, off-putting, fear-inducing, and infuriating for white people to talk about racism.[15]

By expanding the body of research in this area, practitioners will have more resources to help them obtain greater levels of knowledge and sensitivity toward the unequal and oppressive conditions endured by Black and Brown women leaders, including but not limited to workplace bullying due to gender and race, as well as evaluations that are fraught with social dominance orientations.[16]

Why This Discussion Remains Important Today

When the stories and experiences of oppressed peoples are erased, or silenced, deceptions—both for others and themselves—fill the void. As we take a moment to consider the plight of oppressed people in general, and Black and Brown women in particular, understanding the backdrop of our condition is paramount. Understanding how the ghosts of slavery and any variety of forms of oppression lead us to internalized, toxic behaviors and pit us against one another is of supreme importance. Teaching and discussing intersectionality (how race, gender, and class converge to create formidable barriers to opportunities for advancement) remains critical. We must reject the notion that it is somehow a far-left, extreme agenda. To break cycles of dysfunction, hatred, and oppression, we must learn and remember our past.

Black Women—Double Outsiders

Generally speaking, Black women experience double outsider status.[17] Different from white women and Black men, Black women leaders are frequently locked out of informal networks and mentoring relationships that have proved to be advantageous for leadership ascension. Although white women may experience marginalization due to their gender, and Black men may experience oppression due to their race, Black women experience both racism and gender discrimination concurrently. This is what it means to be a double outsider.[18]

Colorism, Biblical Language, and Internalized Racism

Colorism is discrimination based on skin color. Throughout scripture, darkness and light are juxtaposed against one another. Genesis 1:1-5 states:

> In the beginning God created the heavens and the earth. Now the earth was formless and empty, darkness was over the surface of the deep, and the Spirit of God was hovering over the waters.
>
> And God said, "Let there be light," and there was light. God saw that the light was good, and he separated the light from the darkness. God called the light "day," and the darkness he called "night." And there was evening, and there was morning—the first day.

In these verses, God creates light and declares that it is good. He called the light "day" and the darkness "night." This is the first mention of light and darkness in scripture. Jesus describes himself as the Light of the world (John 12:46). God's people are to be lights shining in darkness (Matthew 5:14-16). John 3:19-21 declares that the light has come into the world, the world loves darkness rather than light because their deeds are evil.

Light is associated with holiness. Darkness is associated with evil. Light is associated with God. Darkness is associated with Satan. Nowhere in scripture, however, does God say that dark-skinned people are inherently evil. Neither do any verses support the belief that light-skinned people are inherently godly. However, evil people have used the aforementioned scriptures to suggest that God favors those who are of lighter hues because light/white is associated with purity, cleanliness, enlightenment, and godliness, and darkness/black is associated with filth, evil, ignorance, and sinfulness.

Scripture clearly states that Jesus was Jewish, born in Bethlehem of Judea, and raised in Nazareth of Galilee. Given his ethnic makeup, he more than likely had dark hair, dark brown eyes, and olive-brown colored skin. Yet, Jesus has been consistently depicted as a white man with blue eyes and flowing blondish-gold hair. Imagery is powerful. By using a visual representation of the Son of God as a white man, the message is clear: God is white. God, the "white man" rules over all, is all-powerful, all-seeing, all-knowing, and has determined the order of things in this world. This misinterpretation of scripture lays the groundwork for a plethora of discrimination against people of color in general, and Black people in particular.

America has swung the pendulum back and forth between its dance with diversity, equity, and inclusion. In terms of race, America went from forcing Indigenous people onto reservations, African people into cotton and tobacco fields, and Japanese people into internment camps, to the Reconstruction era when, for a brief period, Black men were able to vote, own land, and hold government offices. Then the pendulum swung the other way. Jim Crow in the South and varying forms of discrimination in the North prevailed. The pendulum swung back as Black people and all United States citizens gained the right to vote, Affirmative Action was instituted, and the middle class became slightly darker in hue. *Roe v. Wade* gave women legalized bodily autonomy, minorities were climbing the economic proverbial ladder, and America elected a Black president.

We blinked, and many of the hard-fought-for rights and privileges we believed we had gained are suddenly being stripped away. Under the Trump Administration, policies that support diversity, equity, and inclusion are being torn down. The conservative Supreme Court overturned *Roe v. Wade*. Affirmative Action has been gutted. Voting rights are under attack, and America's fragile experiment called Democracy teeters on destruction. Amidst all the back and forth, one thing remains consistent. Systems of discrimination remain intact, keeping the door perpetually open to oppress specific groups of people.

Although white women, poor white people, Black men and women, as well as other people of color, experience discrimination, the degrees to which American systems of oppression operate against groups of people differ. Differences in treatment deliberately orchestrated often keep the downtrodden from working together. As one group sees the better treatment of another group, and as groups are ranked based upon certain elusive factors (skin color, ethnicity, geographical location, etc.), anger and hostility against group members of differing groups, rather than the perpetrators, ensues. A divided house cannot stand. Oppressors understand this rule well.

Slave owners used an infamous tactic to separate slaves and their duties by skin color. Mulattos (people of African and European descent) were often given positions as house slaves. They were lighter-skinned and known to be the products of slave masters and the slave women they raped. They served the members of the slave master's family indoors, as maids, butlers, nannies, etc. Darker-skinned men and women were relegated to much harsher labor in the sun-scorched fields. They worked from sunup to sundown with little to no respite. They were prevented from learning to read or write and were severely punished if it was discovered that they knew how to do so.[19]

Lighter-skinned slaves were more appealing to white people and could be sold at a higher price. Mulattos regularly experienced favoritism, not only from their master-fathers but from other whites. Historical records reveal that mulattoes were more likely to gain freedom from white master-fathers, were given greater opportunities to obtain and own land, as well as to gain access to educational opportunities and more lucrative employment.[20]

In his seminal work *Black Bourgeoisie: The Rise of a New Middle Class in the United States,* sociologist E. Franklin Frazier discusses the power of light skin in a Black person's life. From the times of slavery up through the Civil Rights Movement and beyond, light-skinned Blacks were privileged in ways that "darkies" (dark-skinned Black people) were not. They were conditioned to see themselves as better. They married other light-skinned people and passed down the benefits of their complexion to their children.[21] Some mulattos were so fair-skinned that they passed for white. If their skin was light enough, their nose was keen enough, their lips were thin enough, and their hair was straight enough, they just might have appeared white. This was an extremely dangerous road to travel, for if it were discovered that they were Black, they could be killed. Yet, some took this risk for an opportunity to breathe freely and experience nature's passport: white privilege.

I am unsure of the origin of this rhyme, but it was emblematic of the sentiments of many: "If you're white, you're all right; if you're brown, stick around; if you're yellow, you're mellow; if you're Black, step back!" The pain, torture, and anguish of this heinous tactic imposed upon human beings is incomprehensible. Varying hues of people were trained to hate one another. Families were torn apart. Doors to many opportunities were barred and closed. Jealousy, animosity, and envy ran rampant. The plans of the oppressors worked brilliantly.

In addition to using skin color to make differences between slaves, masters used some slaves as semi-overseers. They were not the main overseers—that role was reserved for lower-class white men. The slave overseers would whip, beat, and snitch on slaves who were slacking off in their chores. By using slaves to keep one another down, the purveyors of slavery were largely successful in quelling rebellions and keeping segments of the slave population loyal. Slave owners understood that some crumbs of perceived privilege were better than the abysmal condition of being at the bottom of the caste.

The aforementioned complexion system produced additional pain for Black women. Someone once said that forbidden fruit is the most desirable. Black people were forbidden from looking white people in the eye. Black men were banned from looking at white women. If they were accused of speaking to, looking at, or (God forbid) touching a white woman, they could be tarred and feathered, boiled in a pot of hot water, strung up and hung on a tree, or thrown into a river with a cotton gin anchored around their neck.

White slave owners desired Black slave women and took them whenever they chose. Slaves had no say over their bodies. Masters would send mulatto house workers to the slave quarters and wake slave women out of their beds (as they lay beside their husbands) to go over to the master's appointed place. At times, the master called for the slave woman, not just for his pleasure but for the pleasure of his male house guests. After being sexually abused, ripped, and bloodied, she was sent back to her shack, humiliated, physically and mentally tormented. The white wife was jealous and angry at the Black slave woman. The Black slave man was furious, grieved, and felt emasculated. Neither could do anything about their plight.[22] Many examples of these cruel tactics were explored in Alex Haley's book *Roots* and the biographical series of the same name.[23]

However, white wives and Black slave men had desires of their own. Stories have also been told of the two disenfranchised groups coming together in secret. Black slave men desired white women, and white women desired Black men. Black men, having been used as studs to produce strong offspring for the auction block, intrigued white women, curious about the Black man's sexual prowess.[24]

Years later, following emancipation, some Black men continued to want white women or were drawn to fair-skinned Black women with silky, long hair. They were preferred over dark-skinned, curly, short-haired sisters. Black women began to fight amongst one another. Light-skinned girls experienced bullying, jealousy, and gossip. Dark-skinned girls were laughed at, passed over, and ostracized. Internalized racism had taken root.

The Brown Bag Test and the Blue Vein Societies

During the Jim Crow era, segregation was the law of the land in the South. Most people living today are well aware of the laws that prohibited the races from mixing. Blacks and whites were not allowed to sit in the same areas in restaurants, on various modes of transportation, theatres, churches, public areas, etc. To ensure that no Black person was allowed entrance to any number of places, businesses would use the brown paper bag test. If a person's skin was the same or darker color than a brown paper bag, they were considered Black. Sadly, internalized racism became most prominent following emancipation.

During the mid-1800s, light-skinned Black people formed blue-vein societies.[25] The attitudes that fueled the formation of these societies are an example of *colorism*. In 1982, Alice Walker coined this term to describe how external racism influenced internal racist ideologies among Black people.[26] Much like the brown bag test, if a person's skin was too dark to see that their veins were blue, then they were not permitted to enter the fairer-skinned people's establishments, groups, clubs, sororities, fraternities, etc.[27] How did these behaviors impact Black people in general and Black women in particular? In the words of Ibram X. Kendi, lighter-skinned people are "wealthier, healthier, and more powerful than Dark people."[28]

Although Kendi was referencing realities for Black people in the 1920s, remnants of these realities remain in our society today. Until recent decades (the 2000s up to now), darker-hued Black women were less likely to have lead roles in films, host television shows, receive Academy Awards, anchor news programs, etc. Darker-skinned people were less likely to obtain prominent, well-paid positions, despite levels of experience or education. Black women in particular subjected themselves to scalp-burning, cancer-causing perms to straighten their hair and skin-lightening creams to brighten their complexions and appear more acceptable to everyone, including themselves. However, not everyone ascribed this to self-degradation. During the 1960s, the Black Power movement burst onto the scene. The phrase "Say it Loud. I'm Black and I'm Proud!" became the rallying call of an era.

Vocal artist James Brown codified this saying in his famous song by the same name/phrase.

Black activists, musicians, singers, and even some politicians put down straightening combs and permanents to don afros. They proudly wore large afros and cornrows to highlight their self-acceptance, Black beauty, and pride in their African ancestry. Their natural hairstyles, however, were not accepted by society. Some Black parents warned their youth that they would not be able to gain meaningful employment with "bushy hair" and "undignified" braids.

Unfortunately, for many, the Black parents were correct. Employers, schools, and some establishments would turn away Black people wearing natural hairstyles (afros, braids, cornrows). When Black people did this, they were perceived to be rebels without a cause. Learning much from Civil Rights era strategists, members of the Black community, along with certain businesses such as the powerhouse Dove (skincare) Company, started a national campaign, petitioning Congress to pass legislation striking down such discriminatory practices.

In 2022, their efforts would be rewarded. On Friday, March 18, 2022, the US House, led by the Democrats, passed the CROWN Act, an acronym for "Creating a Respectful and Open World for Natural Hair."[29] Unfortunately, the bill stalled in the Senate and was ultimately defeated as Republicans strongly objected to the bill, declaring that the law already covers this kind of discrimination. However, the current laws *do not* seem to cover this kind of bias against natural hairstyles in practice because people wearing them still experience discrimination.[30] Proponents of the bill are still fighting to get the CROWN Act signed into federal law. The legislation is about more than natural hair. The act also focuses on racial discrimination of all kinds, pay equity, and protections for people of a variety of backgrounds, particularly Black people.[31] The Economic Policy Institute (EPI) reports that over 44 percent of Black women workers live in states where they are at risk for hair-based discrimination.[32]

On a positive note, in 2023, according to the EPI, the CROWN Act is law in Alaska, Arizona, Arkansas, California, Colorado, Connecticut, Delaware, Illinois, Louisiana, Maine, Maryland, Massachusetts, Michigan, Minnesota, Nebraska, Nevada, New Jersey, New Mexico, New York, Oregon, Tennessee, Texas, Virginia, and Washington.[33] Dove also continues to invest significantly in ads that encourage people of all different body types and hues to love the skin that they are in.

How Gender and Race Intersect to Harm Black Women's Health

Crenshaw describes the main tenets of intersectionality theory as understanding social identities as multiple and intersecting.[34] Race, gender, and socioeconomic status intersect with macro-level structural factors such as poverty, racism, career advancement, and sexism to impact every facet of life and health outcomes for Black women.[35] The intersection of gender, race, socioeconomic status, stereotypes, etc., increases harmful stress levels for Black women leaders. Studies show a strong correlation between structural racism and racial health inequalities.[36] Sociologists Danielle D. Dickens, Veronica Y. Womack, and Treshae Dimes discuss the psychological pressure upon Black women in the workplace. Frequently, they are forced to mask their identities to lessen discrimination associated with perceived hyper-blackness.[37]

For example, Black women may change the texture of their hair from curly to straight to appear less threatening. They may strive to alter the cadence of their speech, avoid references to cultural aspects of their everyday life, or remain silent about psychological pain inflicted by frequent verbal microaggressions from white co-workers. Black women also wrestle with identity shifts they may feel pressured to make due to identity stigmatization in the workplace.[38] Each of the aforementioned scenarios is an example of how gender, race, and stereotypes intersect to form systems of oppression for Black women. Intersectionality theory was born out of all these realities.

Black and Brown women are underrepresented in lead and executive-level positions in both the religious and secular realms. When they do gain access, they are frequently appointed to glass cliff situations. Black and Brown women are daunted by unrealistic expectations and stereotypes that stakeholders use to determine the level of their effectiveness. Sadly, the dismantling of racism in our nation has been stymied by a deliberate erasure of history concerning the treatment of people of color in America. For all these reasons, we must hear the lived experiences of oppressed people upon their beings, in their own words. Their voices and insights are necessary for the breaking of unjust and inequitable structures.

Questions and Discussion Starters

Below are questions to help you contemplate, process, and share your thoughts.

1. Share two examples of how false piety and nationalism have been used as tools to erase historical discrimination and oppression in America.
2. Do you agree with banning books? Why or why not?
3. How can individuals, groups, and communities influence institutions of higher learning to increase the employment of Black and Brown women professors? Why is this an important issue?
4. Have you observed or experienced colorism? How did the experience make you feel (either as an observer or a target)?
5. If you have ever experienced racial or gender discrimination, how did it make you feel? What would you

recommend individuals and groups do to help dismantle oppressive, racist systems in America?

NOTES

1. Audre Lorde, "The Master's Tools Will Never Dismantle the Master's House," *Sister Outsider: Essays and Speeches,* 1984, Ed. Berkeley, CA: Crossing Press, 110–114, https://pressbooks.claremont.edu/clas112pomonavalentine/chapter/lorde-audre-the-masters-tools-will-never-dismantle-the-masters-house/.

2. Eunice Choi, "America's history of erasing history," *Princeton Summer Journal,* August 14, 2021, https://princetonsummerjournal.com/2021/08/14/americas-history-of-erasing-history/.

3. Eunice Choi, "America's history of erasing history."

4. Elizabeth A. Harris and Alexandra Alter, "Book bans are rising sharply in public libraries," *New York Times,* https://www.nytimes.com/2023/09/21/books/book-ban-rise-libraries.html (2023).

5. The Community Library & The American Library Association, Band books club: 10 banned books written by Black authors worth reading this Black History Month, (n.d.), https://www.bannedbooksbookclub.com/resources/banned-books-black-history-month-black-authors, https://comlib.org/2022/banned-book-classics/.

6. Douglas Soule and Thao Nguyen, "Florida had more books challenged for removal than any other state in 2023, library organizations say," *USA TODAY*, April 1, 2024, https://www.usatoday.com/story/entertainment/books/2024/04/01/american-library-association-florida-book-challenges/73172976007/.

7. Alex Haley, *Roots: The Saga of an American Family* (Garden City, NY: Doubleday & Co, 1974).

8. Alex Haley, *Roots: The Saga of an American Family.*

9. D. W. Griffith, ed. 1915. *The Birth of a Nation*. Directed by D. W. Griffith, Epoch Producing Co.

10. The Los Angeles Film School, "The history of Black filmmakers who changed Hollywood," *Los Angeles Film School,* n.d., https://www.lafilm.edu/blog/the-history-of-black-filmmakers-who-changed-hollywood/.

11. The Los Angeles Film School, "The history of Black filmmakers who changed Hollywood."

12. Tyler Perry Studios, 2025, https://tylerperrystudios.com/.

13. Grace Adeniyi-Ogunyankin, Moya Bailey, Karen Flynn, Bettina Judd, Anana Weekley, Jennifer Musial, and Melissa White, "Black Feminist Thought and the Gender, Women's, and Feminist Studies PhD: A Roundtable Discussion," *Feminist Formations*, 32, no. 2, 1–28, https://doi.org/10.1353/ff.2020.0023.

14. Adeniyi-Ogunyankin et al., "Black Feminist Thought and the Gender, Women's, and Feminist Studies PhD."

15. Robin DiAngelo, *White Fragility: Why It's So Hard for White People to Talk About Racism* (Boston: Beacon Press, 2020).

16. Christine A. Smith, "Lived Experiences of Inequity of African American Women Leading Struggling, Nonprofit Organizations in the United States: A Phenomenological Study," *Capella University*, 2022, ProQuest Dissertations Publishing, 28964693, 6.

17. LaShonda A. Beckwith, Danon R. Carter, and Tara Peters, "The Underrepresentation of African American Women in Executive Leadership: What's Getting in The Way?" *Journal of Business Studies Quarterly*, 7, no. 4 (2016): 115–134.

18. Christine A. Smith, "Lived Experiences of Inequity of African American Women Leading Struggling, Nonprofit Organizations in the United States: A Phenomenological Study," *Capella University*, 2022, ProQuest Dissertations Publishing, 28964693, 42.

19. Verna Keith and Cedric Herring, "Skin Tone and Stratification in the Black Community," *American Journal of Sociology*, 97 no. 3. (1991): 760–788, http://www.jstor.org/stable/2781783.

20. Keith and Herring, "Skin Tone and Stratification in the Black Community."

21. E. Franklin Frazier, *Black Bourgeoisie: The Rise of a New Middle Class in the United States* (Englewood, NJ: Free Press, 1957).

22. Fay A. Yarbrough, "Power, Perception, and Interracial Sex: Former Slaves Recall a Multiracial South," *The Journal of Southern History* 71, no. 3 (2005): 559–88, https://doi.org/10.2307/27648820.

23. Haley, *Roots*.

24. Yarbrough, "Power, Perception, and Interracial Sex."

25. Bryant, 2001, 74.

26. Keith and Herring, "Skin Tone and Stratification in the Black Community," 250.

27. Ibram X. Kendi, *How to Be an Antiracist* (New York: One World, 2019).

28. Kendi, *How to Be an Antiracist*, 3.

29. Veronica Stracqualursi, "US House Passes CROWN Act That Would Ban Race-Based Hair Discrimination," *CNN*, March 18, 2022, https://www.cnn.com/2022/03/18/politics/house-vote-crown-act/index.html.

30. Stracqualursi, "US House Passes CROWN Act That Would Ban Race-Based Hair Discrimination."

31. Jasmine Patterson-Payne, "The CROWN Act: A Jewel for Combating Racial Discrimination in the Workplace and Classroom," *Economic Policy Institute*, July 26, 2023, https://www.epi.org/publication/crown-act/#:~:text=Notes-,1,2.

32. Patterson-Payne, "The CROWN Act: A Jewel for Combating Racial Discrimination in the Workplace and Classroom."

33. Patterson-Payne, "The CROWN Act: A Jewel for Combating Racial Discrimination in the Workplace and Classroom."

34. Crenshaw, "Demarginalizing the Intersection of Race and Sex: A Black Feminist Critique of Antidiscrimination Doctrine, Feminist Theory and Antiracist Politics."
35. McCluney et al., "Structural racism in the workplace: Does perception matter for health inequalities?"
36. Smith, "Lived Experiences of Inequity of African American Women Leading Struggling, Nonprofit Organizations in the United States," 63.
37. Danielle D. Dickens, Veronica Y. Womack, and Treshae Dimes, "Managing Hypervisibility: An Exploration of Theory and Research on Identity Shifting Strategies in the Workplace Among Black Women," *Journal of Vocational Behavior* 113, 153–163, https://doi.org/10.1016/j.jvb.2018.10.008.
38. Dickens et al., "Managing Hypervisibility."

Section Two

We Shall Overcome—Testimonies and Stories

Earlier in this book, we unpacked the relationship between false piety and power. We explored a variety of ways in which they come together to create and maintain systems that oppress, disenfranchise, and attempt to erase the histories of specific groups of people in America. Now, I want you to hear other voices share their stories. I have invited several of my scholar friends and mentors to provide words of wisdom, insight, testimonies, and stories that can help us overcome. Indeed, we can do exceedingly, abundantly above all that we could ask or think, according to the power that is at work within us (Ephesians 3:20). As this scripture references, this is not the world's power, but God's power of justice, mercy, and humility.

A brother beloved, the Rev. Dr. James C. Perkins, pastor emeritus of Greater Christ Missionary Baptist Church in Detroit, Michigan, and former national president of the Progressive National Baptist Convention (PNBC), will open this broader conversation.

We Shall Overcome—Testimonies and Stories

BY JAMES C. PERKINS

"We Shall Overcome"[1] is a song often sung at the end of our church services or civic meetings. It has been called the anthem of the Civil Rights Movement. Those courageous souls sang this song while they marched into the face of danger, protesting the laws of segregation and discrimination that prevented them from participating as full citizens in this society. It is futuristic and aspirational: We *shall* overcome . . . It expresses the hopes and aspirations of our forebears that one day we would be free from the burden of white supremacy, racism, sexism, and oppression of any kind.

On several occasions, I have had young people ask me, "Why do we need to sing this song? It's too slow, and it sounds like slave music." To which I have tried to explain how closely connected it is to our history and struggle as a people. Our young people do not know what it means to be Black in America. Yet as I pen these words, the recently elected president, who has been in office a mere three days, has already issued executive orders to eliminate voting rights, DEI programs, and plans to deport refugees who have come to this land seeking to build a better life.

Our young people do not have the historical foundation to understand what all of this means. And as the Black church, it is our responsibility to teach them. Like no other time in our long, historic march toward justice and equality, we find ourselves on the brink of losing every social, economic, and political gain we have made since we landed on these pristine shores. Like no other time in our history, we need to come together as a people.

We need to come together as an *activist church*. The old saints used to call it "the Church militant." They recognized that we are not just fighting against social aberrations. We are engaged in spiritual warfare. We're in a battle between good and evil, right and wrong, between truth and lies. We need the Black church to align with the will of the God of justice and be at the center of determining what kind of future our people will have. That was the objective of those who marched singing, "We shall overcome!"

They had resilience and determination to fight against the evil of injustice for as long as it took. Racism, sexism, economic injustice, and other forms of oppression are systemic. The election of a Black president does not mean the end of these evils. We learned this from the election of President Barack Obama. There has been a strong resurgence of racism as a backlash to our progress. It means that, once again, we have come to a crossroads in American life where our nation has a choice.

Will we choose to go forward into a future where every person has the right and opportunity to live up to their God-given potential, or will we continue to be possessed by the demons of the past, where racism, injustice, and exploitation are the ruling forces in our lives? Professor Walter Wink refers to this as the domination system. It consists of three components: political oppression, economic exploitation, and religious legitimation. Unfortunately, white Christianity has always used religion to justify its oppressive systems. This is true today. This is what they mean by white Christian nationalism. They (white Christian nationalists) believe that the government ought to tell the church what it can and cannot do.

They are trying to establish a theocratic authoritarian form of government where they define who God is and what it means to be a Christian. They call themselves Christian, but as Professor Jim Wallis says, "They're really more white than Christian."[2] So as wonderful as it was that we had a Black woman presidential candidate for the first time (in the person of Vice President Kamala Harris), we quickly learned that the struggle is not over. We must be vigilant and faithful to the struggles of the past.

We must continue to engage in the political process because it is by electing people who understand our struggle for justice and who share our values and our hopes that policies are established that transform the system. The system should look like the one Jesus described when He said, "For I was hungry and you gave me something to eat, I was thirsty and you gave me something to drink, I was a stranger and you invited me in, I needed clothes and you clothed me, I was sick and you looked after me, I was in prison and you came to visit me" (Matthew 25:35-36). Only when the system has been transformed can we sing, "We *have* overcome." We have got to instill our history and this spiritual purpose and power into our youth so they too will strive to overcome, and sing as they strive, *WE SHALL OVERCOME!*

Until that day, keep on praying, keep on hoping, keep on fighting, keep on singing, "We **shall** overcome."

NOTES

1. In the public domain.
2. Samuel Smith, 2017 "Jim Wallis: People Upset over NFL Anthem Protests Are More 'White' than 'Christian,'" *Christian Post*, October 8, 2017, https://www.christianpost.com/news/jim-wallis-people-upset-over-nfl-anthem-protests-are-more-white-than-christian.html.

CHAPTER 5
The Politics of the Powerful

You may recall from previous chapters the tactics of those who benefit from colonialism and the proponents of racist and sexist power structures. What are some of the ways that those tactics have conditioned oppressed people to perpetuate their own oppression? I share some of my own reflections on these issues. Then, two of my colleagues, sisters, and friends will share their personal experiences and offer valuable insights into the politics of the powerful.

A Different Perspective on the Parable of the Talents—My (Chris's) Personal Reflection

I have always been challenged by the Parable of the Ten Talents (or minas). My challenge had less to do with the nobleman's rights and more with the man who took his talent and hid it in the ground. Why would he do such a thing? Why did he dig a hole and hide the money in the ground?

A few years ago, I went through a struggle (really an emotional crisis) as the pastor of a small congregation. While the people I serve are loving, supportive, and trusting of my leadership (all things that I do not take for granted), we lack strong infrastructure in terms of human resources. Many responsibilities end up back in the pastor's lap even when delegated. Despite amazing guest speakers, workshops, Bible studies, and teaching, church growth efforts lagged as the members have not been particularly evangelistic in nature. Most outreach efforts fall to the work of the pastor. I felt weary, wounded, and sad. I felt daunted and frustrated.

This is not unique to me, personally. Many of my female pastor colleagues struggle through this same or a similar situation. As previously discussed, there is an uptick in the number of Black women pastors who are being embraced by Black churches and becoming senior pastors of healthier congregations. For this, we give God praise! The double-edged sword of this praise report is that people believe that the struggle is over, and the aforementioned circumstances are no longer an issue. Women in general and Black women, in particular, still comprise only a fraction of the number of senior pastors, even more true of economically stable, strong infrastructure congregations. Although women make up a majority of members in churches in general and Black churches in particular, women have been conditioned to follow male leadership. Many women prefer a male pastor to a female pastor. I discuss this at length in my first book, *Beyond*.[1]

Okay, I digress. As I lamented before the Lord concerning my plight, I was inspired to revisit the Parable of the Talents. Something I had read numerous times jumped out at me in a new way. I heard the Holy Spirit say, "If I choose to only give you one, e.g., this one small congregation, are you going to dig a proverbial hole in the ground and not do your best with what you have? Will you ignore all that I have given you and remain focused on what you do not have? Look at what is in your hand and use it for God's glory!" That day, my heart, mind, and vision for the work of the ministry God has entrusted to my care were transformed.

The sin of the servant in the text was not having little. The sin was neglecting to use the little that was given. With this fresh perspective, I emerged from the depths of despair. Out of that struggle was birthed a beautiful, influential, exemplary ministry of collaboration. The workers in our church have grown slightly, but the magnitude of the work that we have been able to do has expanded exponentially. Our look has changed from inward to outward. We regularly collaborate with other congregations, educational institutions, hospitals, and community agencies to minister to children, youth, and adults. Has our situation changed? Not really. Has our perspective changed? Absolutely! God has taken our little and made it much!

Just as God gave me a new revelation about this text, my dear friend and sister Rev. Gimbiya Kettering also offers a new perspective on this same text. I invite you to join me in hearing her heart and contemplating her understanding of this passage. Within the context of discrimination, racism, and oppression, her insights challenge us to look again and see new possibilities.

* * * * * * * * * * * * * * *

The Parable of the Foreign King

Rev. Gimbiya Kettering, co-author of *Reparations and the Theological Disciplines: Prophetic Voices for Remembrance, Reckoning, and Repair*;[2] former Director of Intercultural Ministries, Church of the Brethren; writer; and workshop leader, focused on the intersections of race, religion, and political policy

> Jesus said: "A man of noble birth went to a distant country to have himself appointed king and then to return. So he called ten of his servants and gave them ten minas.
> 'Put this money to work,' he said, 'until I come back.'
> But his subjects hated him and sent a delegation after him to say,
> 'We don't want this man to be our king.'"—Luke 19:12-14

If you are me, you are a little Black girl in a predominantly white church. You are just beginning to realize that you are different, and you will spend the rest of your life parsing how much of this difference is because you are not white and how much is because you do not want a king. For now, your mother prepares you for church by blowdrying your hair straight and then plaiting it. She makes you wear pleated, floral dresses with wide lace collars.

Your resistance is as futile as her attempts to help you fit in. During these Sunday preparations, one or both of you will cry, and harsh words will be exchanged. You are only a little girl with tangly hair in clothes that make you feel like you do not belong to yourself, and you do not yet have those words to ask her if the intent is camouflage or assimilation. It is the difference between seeking fortification and claiming reformation.

Despite this hair regime and strict dress code, the Sunday school teacher looks at you like you are a goat among sheep. In the coloring sheets she passes out, Jesus and Moses and Mary and the disciples have hair that flows downward. Despite how you fight your mother's hot blowdryer, you do want flowing hair. Sunday school lessons are repetitive: the lifecycle of Jesus, a selection of safe prophets, predictable miracles, and the agricultural parables, including the lost sheep, the seeds, the fig tree. Despite the bland predictability, you pay attention. Of course, there is the Parable of the Talents. Your confusion starts because you think that a talent is a *talent.*

The people of your church, predominantly white, are good people who want to be responsible Christians who multiply the glory of God. Their faith is interwoven with their bleached American story about coming up by the bootstraps, investment ingenuity, and individual achievement. They await the affirmation from their master, *well done, my good and faithful servant*. These words ring in your bones too, but even as a little girl these foundations of faith and prosperity feel like sinking sand.

If you are me, a little Black girl who does not sing, nor play the piano, nor cartwheel, you cannot juggle. You finish races last, and you do not knit, nor crochet, nor embroider. You are, in the talents of childhood and expectations of womanhood, talentless. Even your handwriting is horrible. And it is not fair that the servant, who did not lose anything, did not steal anything, did not hurt anyone, is publicly shamed for returning what was given to him. Talents that he had never even asked for. Your heart has as many questions as a drum has beats.

When you raise your hand, the Sunday school teacher looks at you as if you are an unworthy servant who has done nothing with your talents. Or maybe her look is that of a tired woman who only wants to finish the worksheets, practice the song for next Sunday, and give everyone a snack. Your church says that women can be pastors, but you have never seen a woman in the pulpit. Someday, you will be a woman working for the church and your memory will be kinder to your volunteer Sunday school teacher. Maybe hers was the look of a woman who wanted to be paid for her hermeneutical talents instead of being smothered by the expectation to give back in the womanly domains of hearth, home, and unruly children who are unclear about the difference between wealth and the gifting of aptitudes. When she nods at you, you say what is on your heart. "But it is not fair . . ."

You were only a talentless little girl, and your memories are blurry. You do not remember if you explained to her that you were confused because you thought God was just and generous. Why would a God who looked after the lost sheep and fed the hungry take away a talent? Something about this feels unfair and wrong. You do not yet have the courage to ask what it means that you do not have a talent. You console yourself with the belief that if you have not been given a talent, then you will owe the master nothing. Even if you cannot yet talk about false piety and hypocrisy, this seed of doubt is also the seed of your liberation.

* * *

In Luke 19, the Parable of the Talents comes after the story of Zacchaeus, another story mismanaged by the Sunday school teachers who focused on his stature and not his promise of reparations. It recontextualizes the parable when one realizes it follows a testimony of a conversion that returns ill-gotten gains and repentance for collaboration with the empire. Furthermore, Jesus tells the parable because he senses the crowd's anticipation that *he is near Jerusalem, and the people think the kingdom of God will appear at once.*

Jesus, of the tribe Judah, one of the peoples whose land had been claimed by an expanding, foreign empire, had to tell them that he would not bring the kingdom these people imagined. He did not come with legionnaires and chariots; there would be no great battle and no crowning of a new king. So, Jesus told them a parable about the master as a nobleman, hated by his own people, traveling to claim regency over an Indigenous people and their land. For the first people hearing the story, they would have noticed that the servant, oppressed and frightened, who resisted the master, did not have a happy ending.

But we, most of us in the American Christian tradition, have heard the parable as a warning against laziness. We mythologize a Puritan work ethic. We make hay while the sun shines and keep our noses to the grindstone. We endure the daily grind and the rat race. We focus on what the servant did not do instead of listening to why the servant refused to make the hard, vengeful king wealthier. We are, in the measures of the world, a wealthy nation, too often hard on servants and demanding stratospheric returns on our investment. Too often, as if seeking age-appropriate Sunday school lessons, we abridge the parable so it stops short of verses the servant's confession:

"He also who had received the one talent came forward, saying, 'Master, I knew you to be a hard man, reaping where you did not sow, and gathering where you scattered no seed, so I was afraid, and I went and hid your talent in the ground. Here, you have what is yours'" (Matthew 25:24-25; Luke 19:20-21, ESV).

We do not LISTEN to the man who explains why he will not use his talent to enrich the king. Even after we have witnessed Zacchaeus's repentance, we cannot understand we have reparations to make. For us, a nation that has built wealth on a doctrine of discovery and enslavement, the Parable of the Talents offers a metaphor for colonialization: a foreigner claiming sovereignty to discovered lands, the ethnic groups divided against one another like servants, and multiplication of the minas illustrates the exploitation of labor and the extraction of natural resources. But we prefer the echo of affirmation when President John F. Kennedy said, *those to whom great things are given, great things are demanded.*[3] And we await the great battle that will set up a new worldly kingdom in which we shall be the great ones.

As a child, when the parable ended with the frightened, truthful servant being cast into the place of wailing and gnashing of teeth, you imagined the hold of a ship on the Middle Passage. Or perhaps it was the other way around: As you began to understand the magnitude of the Middle Passage, you imagined being packed below deck and you imagined the servant resisting a hard, vengeful master.

* * *

At the end of Luke 19, the hope for a new kingdom is at once realized and undone as unarmed and unaccompanied, Jesus rides a donkey into the Holy City. An animal intended for farmwork, like the crown of thorns, makes a mockery of the trappings of monarchy. Instead of a violent revolution, we are reminded our treasure is still in heaven, not on Earth, the house has rooms enough for everyone, the true talents are the gifts of the spirit, and the greatest of these is always love. Palm Sunday, as we call this story, turns upside down and inside out what it means to be wealthy, to be powerful, to have done well before a God of justice.

It took me decades to understand that the master of every parable is not God. Just as often, Christ warns us about the dangers of earthly masters such as slave owners and overseers, genocidaires who stole land from those they killed, corporate raiders who want to reap profits in companies where they do not work, and the promoters of multilevel marketing schemes that leave people broken by debt–hard, feared masters. Likewise, in the stories of America, a conquering nation and economic empire, I am not just a servant, but also the resistance and the survivor. I have had to learn to live on land that was not meant for me, as I retell the stories of America to include me. I resist scriptural interpretations that would cast aside anyone for telling the truth, for being afraid, for being a servant.

As I had suspected as a child, life is not fair. It is not the servant who has wronged the master, but the master who has wronged the servant. In America, I am the descendant of the wronged servant. I am part of the delegation that comes with the news, *we do not want that man to be our king.* I let my natural hair curl, and learning to love my hair means loving my mother, who kept me safe from servitude in the best ways she knew. It means reading the womanist theology of Hagar. It means the imperfect repentance of living on stolen land with the nightmares of my ancestors and the dreams of my children.

To you, the little girl with her raised hand, I whisper, *this is your talent.*

* * * * * * * * * * * * * * *

Give Honor to Whom Honor Is Due—A Personal Testimony (Chris)

For the first five years of serving as a senior pastor, I also served as a part-time hospital chaplain. At that time, the pastoral care staff was predominantly white. There was one other Black chaplain on staff, who was a man. During one of our weekly staff meetings, our pastoral care director led us in a conversation on the importance of honoring elder Black patients by calling them "Mr. So and So . . . Ms. So and So." The conversation was necessary because some of our white chaplains were entering hospital rooms of Black men and women twice or more their age, calling them by their first names.

It appears that they did not know or understand the shameful history of disrespect Black people endured during and after slavery in America. No matter how old a Black person was, or how young a white person was, they would call Black men "boy" and Black women "girl." When they were not referencing them as the n-word, they would call them by whatever name they felt like using that day—Tom, Joe, Sally, or Sue. They did not care what their names were because, to them, they were less than human, more akin to beasts.

Names are important. For many cultures, the name that a child is given reflects aspects of character, faith, strength, courage, and lineage. It is insulting to ignore a person's name or intentionally mispronounce it deliberately. This history was critical for our pastoral care staff to understand. Being in the hospital can be a humiliating experience for anyone. When being made to wear gowns that expose the backside, having strangers bathe you, examine you, poke and prod you, etc., being identified with the appropriate honorific or title is important. For people who have been consistently disrespected, degraded, and humiliated, respect is an important thing.

This is well understood in the Black church. We do not call our pastors "Jim, Sam, Bob." We call them "Reverend Jones, Pastor Williams, Dr. Johnson, Bishop Stokes." Our deacons are "Deacon Jones." Our women are "Sister, or Mother, or Elder." The Black church has struggled over many years to honor our women pastors and preachers with the same respect given to the men. To God be the glory, Black women have come a long way in terms of having our gifts and calling recognized. Many Black churches now have women who serve as associate ministers and have the title of reverend. We also have churches that have moved from the created name and office of deaconess (the wife of a male deacon), to ordaining women as deacons (meaning servant). Yes, we should not be hung up on titles, EXCEPT when all the men in the room are called, "Reverend, Pastor, Doc, and Bishop," and the woman (who frequently has an earned title) is called "Sister So and So," or "Mary."

Women are frequently counseled to ignore the disrespect—"You know who you are . . . you are working for the Lord, not man . . . just keep on serving and the Lord will lift you up." At what point do we straighten our backs, stand up, and say, "ENOUGH!"?

Below, another dear sister colleague shares her experiences with saying, "Enough!" and "being enough."

* * * * * * * * * * * * * * *

My Experiences with Persons in Power Structures in America

Rev. Dr. TaNikka Sheppard, Executive Minister, The Cleveland Baptist Association; Acting General Secretary, North American Baptist Fellowship

In America, we have very destructive definitions of power and limited conceptions of how to use it. Power is often viewed as an addictive notion of authority, too frequently measured by how much control one has over others or how many people one dominates. Unfortunately, this mindset permeates every area of our society, especially in faith-based spaces, where success is often mismeasured not by the souls and lives that are transformed, but by the number of bodies over which one has influence and domination.

As a Christian, I have always believed that I am called to be countercultural. For many years, I frequently quoted Audre Lorde, who said, "The master's tools will never dismantle the master's house. They may allow us temporarily to beat him at his own game, but they will never enable us to bring about genuine change."[4] This was one of my favorite mantras until I realized, to my great disappointment, that most people I know, even those who consider themselves to be activists or social justice advocates, are not truly trying to dismantle "the master's house." In fact, they're just trying to build and maintain their own versions of it. In my experience, one can unknowingly get entangled in other people's proverbial "plantation dreams." Furthermore, if someone is as idealistic as I was, simply trying to serve humanity, honor God, and make the world a better place, they will be easily taken advantage of because of the internalization of repressive ideals that are particularly harmful to women and people of color. It's dangerous in America for Black women to idealize servanthood, and in some ways, even servant leadership.

I remember reading *Their Eyes Were Watching God* by Zora Neale Hurston when I was in high school. I've never forgotten the classic statement of one of the characters who said, "The Black woman is the mule of the world."[5] Mules are burden bearers. They do tireless work while others take credit for their accomplishments, and nobody truly thanks mules, besides giving them a pat on the head, a short rest, or a treat. Then the mules are immediately set back to work because their value is based on their ability to undertake hard and heavy labor, no matter the harshness of the conditions or hazards to their health.

As a Black woman in Christian leadership, I have been encouraged and celebrated for "muling." Yet, the reality is that my personhood is among the most devalued in America, where the ideal personification of leadership is a white man. I'm often treated as a problematic paradox because I'm the exact opposite of who people desire as their leader—I am neither white nor a man. It's an arduous existence because I've had to work twice as hard and have still not received equitable pay, respect, or authority.

Furthermore, my years of "muling" caused me to believe that my identity and value were based on my tireless labor, not my character, capacities, intellect, personality, or creativity. These qualities were only valuable insofar as they could be commodified and used to support those in power. Although these notions weren't always explicitly stated, I was conditioned to step back and relinquish power by observing what was celebrated, criticized, and ostracized. I observed the intense criticism directed at women who sought or occupied leadership positions, as if they were intruding into areas not intended for them. These experiences influenced my perception of which roles were considered suitable or unsuitable for me to pursue. This was exacerbated by watching my male colleagues receive mentoring, support, and learning experiences that were never offered to me or other women.

Throughout the years, I have fought to circumvent these limitations, but such efforts were not without consequences. During this process, relationships were irrevocably altered. Some leaders who initially supported and applauded my rise and resilience resisted my authority. They tried to control my progress as if they owned my abilities because they had aided my development. This "ownership mentality" is one of the "master's tools" that I often witness being wielded in leadership spaces. To prevail, I had to mentally and emotionally liberate myself from the restrictions of their disapproval and demands. Exercising my free will, autonomy, and agency brought criticism and condemnation that hurt. However, the ongoing regret of not excelling was worse. So, I learned to step forward rather than retreat.

Stepping up ignited new ongoing struggles. As a Black woman in America, having leadership and authority doesn't guarantee equitable treatment. We have to fight for it. Often, we don't receive what we deserve, but we sometimes gain what we negotiate for. Hopefully, one day, we'll obtain what we stand up for, but nothing is given. I have faced a lifetime of limiting beliefs and assumptions of my ignorance, in which nearly every decision I made was questioned or challenged. People assume because I'm Black, or because I'm a woman, that they have to teach me something. I've actually been in meetings where I've been called "girl" or "young lady," but not in a way that was affirming or jesting. These were power plays, methods of reminding me that, in their eyes, I did not belong and would not be respected.

Eventually, such interactions took a toll on my joy and mental strength, causing me to be in a consistent state of unease. In my early thirties, I had high blood pressure because I was habitually working so hard, always anxious, and constantly trying to prove myself. Those experiences built a mounting fear and anxiety in me that developed into a pursuit of perfectionism, sometimes driving me crazy with tedious toiling and other times immobilizing me with indecisiveness.

Thankfully, I eventually discovered the value of ignoring people's ignorance, choosing my battles wisely, and redefining "good work." To survive, I've also learned to navigate the treacherous innuendos and microaggressions of racist misogyny to find my own voice and use it to speak up for myself and others. While fighting, I make sure to protect my joy, shield my time, and maintain a sense of balance in my life. I fight to live the best life that I can without it being taken away.

I have learned to embrace my accomplishments without feeling embarrassed. Simultaneously, I learned to accept my failures, treating them as valuable lessons and significant teachers. God, counseling, and friends have helped me overcome the strictures of false humility. It has taken me years to come out of a mindset that conditioned me to suppress my voice, my light, my dreams, my hope, and really, the totality of who I am. Even now, my most profound act of defiance is to embrace myself as I am, rather than how I wish to be. I cherish and accept myself as sufficient and worthy, asserting my place in authoritative spaces without succumbing to the pressure of overworking to justify my presence.

Finally, as an American, I had to recognize my own participation in these toxic power paradigms. Even those of us who champion equity and justice still participate as beneficiaries of others' suffering. While doing so, we live in blissful ignorance of the unbearable working conditions of many of the people who harvest our food or make our clothes. Sadly, most of us internalize these horrendous paradigms that teach us that the conditions of our birth automatically make us superior and entitle us to preferential treatment. Being educated, recognizing the wrongness of our systems, and feeling bad about them are not enough. Repentance, followed by righteous action, is required to be just. While I may not be able to change the systems, I can change how I engage with them and how I teach others to navigate them as well.

* * * * * * * * * * * * * * *

I am grateful to the friends and mentors who transparently shared their experiences with "isms" and abusive power structures. Each of their stories allows us to reflect upon systems and structures that harm many through injustice. Their stories also provide us with inspiration and encouragement—collective experiences that can help us believe that we can do exceedingly, abundantly above all that we could ask or think, according to the power that is at work within us (inspired by Ephesians 3:20). The power this scripture references is not the world's power but God's power of justice, mercy, and humility.

Questions and Discussion Starters

Below are questions to help you contemplate, process, and share your thoughts.

1. Which one stood out to you the most from the testimonies shared? In what ways can you relate?

2. Have you ever felt like "digging a hole" for something you felt was not good or couldn't make a difference? Share an example.
3. Share ways in which we can be intentional about showing respect to others.
4. How can individuals stand with individuals who say, "Enough"?
5. Why are these important discussions for the church and society?

NOTES

1. Christine A. Smith, *Beyond the Stained Glass Ceiling: Equipping and Encouraging Female Pastors* (Judson Press, 2013).

2. Michael Drew Barram, Gimbiya Kettering, and Michael J. Rhodes, *Reparations and the Theological Disciplines* (Rowman & Littlefield, 2023).

3. "Increased responsibility goes with increased ability, for 'of those to whom much is given, much is required.'" Remarks in Nashville at the 90th Anniversary Convocation of Vanderbilt University (192), May 18, 1963, Public Papers of the Presidents: John F. Kennedy, 1963. (President Kennedy was quoting from Luke 12:48) John F. Kennedy Presidential Library and Museum. 2019. "John F. Kennedy Quotations | JFK Library," 2019, https://www.jfklibrary.org/learn/about-jfk/life-of-john-f-kennedy/john-f-kennedy-quotations.

4. Audre Lorde, "The Master's Tools Will Never Dismantle the Master's House," *Sister Outsider: Essays and Speeches*, 1984, Ed. Berkeley, CA: Crossing Press, 110–114, https://pressbooks.claremont.edu/clas112pomonavalentine/chapter/lorde-audre-the-masters-tools-will-never-dismantle-the-masters-house/.

5. Zora Neale Hurston, *Their Eyes Were Watching God* (Philadelphia, PA: J. B. Lippincott, 1937).

CHAPTER 6

Sexism, Racism, and Glass Cliffs (Testimonies)

So God created mankind in his own image, in the image of God he created them; male and female he created them.
—*Genesis 1:27*

Girls are not objects, how dare you objectify us and talk about our bodies as if we're sexual objects? WE ARE NOT! What you have done is cyber-bullying and sexual harassment. I was not a victim of the list but I AM A GIRL and I HATE MISOGYNY. I want our voices to be heard.
—ARIS SMITH, WRITTEN AS A HIGH SCHOOL SOPHOMORE FOLLOWING A SOCIAL MEDIA POST WHERE ANONYMOUS BOYS RELEASED "BRACKETS," A PROCESS WHERE BOYS RANK GIRLS BASED UPON THEIR PHYSICAL APPEARANCE.[1]

Early in my doctoral studies, I decided that I wanted to better understand the experiences of women in general and Black women in particular as they led struggling, non-profit organizations. To do so, I engaged in phenomenology, a research process that seeks the deeper meaning of a phenomenon. Basically, I interviewed specific individuals on multiple occasions to identify the psychological meanings behind their lived experiences.

I asked my study participants to describe their experiences of inequity as leaders of organizations, and then I examined their responses using Crenshaw's Intersectionality Theory. As you may remember from earlier, intersectionality theory argues that race, gender, and class intersect to create formidable systemic barriers for Black women (as well as certain other minority women) across a variety of sectors. Intersectionality theory emphasizes the reality that interlocking systems create barriers that seek to delegitimize the voices, experiences, and ideologies of Black women.[2]

To learn more about the experiences of those in the study, I asked them to describe the role of race and gender in their leadership roles. As discussed previously, minority women are frequently called to lead glass cliff organizations—organizations that may be considered to be struggling, unstable, and dysfunctional. The glass cliff may also be an appointment to an economically stable organization with a toxic, dysfunctional, racist, and or sexist environment.

Every participant was a Black woman between the ages of forty and seventy-five. They had served as leaders in one or more organizations for between five and twenty-six years. They had led both religious and secular organizations. I noticed three predominant themes as I looked at what the women had in common:

- Inequity and Associated Feelings
- Common Internal Response Patterns
- Mental Processes and Coping

Participants openly and transparently shared their inner experiences and emotions evoked by their perceptions of inequities in their workplaces. For some, the wounds from micro and macro aggressions experienced were fresh. For others, they were a more distant memory, but scars remained. I believe you will find their experiences and insights poignant. To protect their confidentiality, I use pseudonyms to help tell their stories. Sadly, younger women, who were not a key focus of this study, also expressed feelings of anger, pain, and frustration over being objectified by young men in their high school. It is important to consider how a "boys just being boys" mentality lays the foundation for sexist behaviors in young men as they grow older.

Black Women Working in "Traumatized Spaces"

Bright, energetic, filled with vision and great possibilities, Mary was the head of communications for a non-profit organization. She directed all phases of production for the company newsletters, email communications, special announcements, etc. She led a team of reporters and volunteers and was responsible for enhancing the company's branding. In addition to her job, she was recently separated from her husband and was raising her two elementary school-age girls.

Despite her responsibilities at home and on the job, she became a multitasking master. Notwithstanding her challenging tasks, she did her work with excellence. But like many women working in male-dominated spaces and being one of a few Black people in leadership, her coworkers second-guessed her directives, passed over her ideas in meetings, and rarely applauded her contributions. The words she used to describe her experience in that role were:

Inequity	Anger	Confusion
Invisibility	Frustration	Trauma
Stress		

She described her work environment as a "traumatized space." When asked to elaborate, Mary described the traumatized space as "just learned to cope . . . just kept going . . . You know, that's what we do. African American women, we make our way out of no way. You know, we do our work and do it to the best of our ability. We go early and stay late. We share our voice, you know, we're representing the room. We try to look good, but oftentimes, we don't feel good."

After sharing additional experiences, Mary ended by saying, "I compartmentalize it, you know, you would never hear me talk about trauma. You will never hear me talk about being in the traumatized space. I was glad to be in the room. The trauma of being mistreated by things, race, and gender that go beyond you. They're kinda like the elephant in the room."

Mary's experience is not unique. Unfortunately, many and varied struggles experienced by Black women leaders related to their racial and gendered identities have been largely ignored in management research.[3] Though *visible* (able to be physically seen) due to the color of their skin, they remain *invisible* (essentially ignored) in terms of their ideas, opportunities for promotion, inequitable treatment, and the silencing of their voices.[4]

Sharon shared her experience of feeling invisible when she had to continue to introduce herself to two white colleagues whom she had previously met on several occasions. She shared, "You know how you've met a person for the first time and then the next time you see them, you're 'seeing' them, you're not 'meeting' them. But apparently, I'm so insignificant or forgettable to these people, and it's, 'Oh, I'm so and so,' when we just did this a month ago."

Pam experienced constant belittlement and second-guessing of her decisions as she worked as a leader in a nonprofit organization. Pam shared, "There were many instances where I felt belittled when using my wisdom. Like always being second-guessed, questions about everything. There was always this sense of doubting my decision-making . . . things of that nature. Doubting my decision-making. Yes. Like questioning everything that I would do."

Psychological educator and writer Stephanie Pappas argues that racist stressors are persistent and can advance toward becoming racial trauma for individuals. Additionally, data reveal the physiological and economic toll workplace inequities cause for Black women leaders.[5] Stress levels due to workplace discrimination can produce harmful results not only for individuals but by creating toxic work environments for all involved. Studies show a strong correlation between structural racism and racial health inequalities.[6]

Some participants described stress and physical pain intensifying as they worked in inequitable spaces. Mary described it like this: "I remember navigating physical space in this place, daily in pain, physical pain trying to do my job to the best of my ability, trying to be seen and wanting to be promoted."

On a positive note, all three of these women ultimately left those toxic "traumatized" spaces and gained employment in more positive work arenas. Not to be underestimated, however, is the impact on a person's health, self-esteem, finances, and career trajectory.

After leaving a toxic environment or traumatized space, women may need some time to bounce back. The voices of doubt and negativity from other people are draining, spirit-crushing, and dangerous. Constantly having your decisions second-guessed can and will cause you to second-guess yourself. Some people may accept a lower-paying job to escape the toxicity of their former work situation. Some successfully navigate this labyrinth of dysfunction. Others do not. I have personally known Black women who have been hired as a news director, an executive director, a senior pastor of a prominent, economically stable church, and a hospital CEO. We celebrated their ascension to these high-level positions. We invited them to be our guest speakers for special days. We asked them to write references for us as we pursued higher heights! Only, we would learn six months later, three years later, or five years later that the organization or church that hired or called them to those positions concluded "they were not a good fit" or their excellent work suddenly became "less than" in the organization's eyes.

I have watched some of those same brilliant, vision-filled, AMAZING women be cut down, thrown into economic peril, become physically sick, and literally die. No one is perfect.

These women certainly were not. However, we have all observed minimally experienced, lacking-in-skill, ill-prepared men and majority-culture people being given high-paying, high-level positions. To add insult to injury, many times, women and minorities are called upon to train them, teach them, catch their mistakes, and cover their backs. All of these are examples of Intersectionality Theory, systemic racism, and sexism in action.

Coping, Giving Grace, and Forgiveness

Historically, spirituality has been a foundational source of strength and coping within the Black community. Black people are not a monolith. We have observed a variety of faith traditions and belief systems, which we embrace. The role of Christianity, specifically in the Black church, has anchored Black people and given them a spirit of resiliency amid racism, oppression, and social hostility.

Akin to prayer and faith are the concepts of giving grace and forgiveness. People of faith tend to view forgiveness through the lens of grace and mercy. In other words, it is not that the person committing the offense deserves forgiveness. It is an act of mercy because God forgave us of our sins. In the words of Jesus, "Forgive us our debts as we forgive our debtors" (Matthew 6:12, KJV). In the words of Mahatma Gandhi, "An eye for an eye will leave the whole world blind."[7] Some participants offered both forgiveness and grace to those who hurt them through racist and sexist behaviors. In addition to faith, prayer, and forgiveness, women need to know that it is okay to embrace their feelings of hurt, anger, and disappointment. We need to be able to plop our feelings out on the proverbial table, look at them, process them, and decide the best and healthiest path forward. That path may include visiting a counselor, therapist, pastor, or a well-vetted confidant. Stuffing emotions by denying they exist will set us up for both mental and physical illness in the long run. Avoid suffering in silence. Get it out. Make a plan. Move ahead.

These stories highlight the reality that Black women experience workplaces differently than majority culture women and men based on their ethnicity, class, and social environment.[8] Hearing the experiences of minority women in their voices can help organizational leaders develop strategies to transform workplaces. Learning from their insights can also help other women leaders and the organizations they serve determine to diminish inequities, remove barriers, and level the playing field.

Redirecting the Next Generation

Earlier, I shared a quote from my daughter, Aris Smith. At the time, she was a sophomore in high school. I remember her coming home one day extremely upset. When I asked what had happened, she shared with me that young men in the school had put together a list, ranking girls in the school based on their bodies and their looks. She explained that some of the girls in the school were crying, devastated because they ranked low on the list. Some girls were outraged (as they should be) because what the boys did was ugly, insensitive, and misogynistic. Although not on the list, Aris joined the girls in their angry protests against the mean-spirited foolishness. They decided to submit an article to the school's online newsletter, *The Shakerite,* which featured Aris's quote.

The article titled, "More than a Ranking: In the face of discrimination, women across Shaker Heights unite and tell their stories in support."[9] Girls throughout the school took a stand. I was proud to see how these young women claimed their agency, stood up, spoke up, and used their voices to make a difference. We must teach young women the importance of valuing their voices, not just their bodies, using their minds and not just their sex appeal, and advocating for others, not just themselves.

We must also teach our young men that women are not a *thing* to be used for pleasure. We must teach them to treat them with respect, listen to them, exchange ideas with them, and value their voices, all while admiring their beauty. Women are not creatures to be lorded over or controlled. They are equal partners with gifts, skills, talents, ideas, strengths, weaknesses, challenges, hopes, and dreams—just as boys and men are. We must not condone, ignore, or excuse ugly, sexist, demeaning, abusive behaviors by repeating the ill-informed mantra, "Boys will be boys." We are better than that.

When we choose to endorse, condone, encourage, and excuse the mistreatment of girls by boys, we are teaching girls that sexist, abusive behaviors are just how boys let you know that they like you. We, in turn, are also teaching boys that these behaviors are acceptable masculine behaviors. They may even think these are ways of showing who is in charge or even sexy. These descriptors may sound over the top, but not really. Television shows, streaming programs, movies, and social media platforms frequently feature "bad boys," who are rough, tough womanizers, who are in some instances abusive. Some young women long for attention and affection and are conditioned to find these behaviors attractive. They have no idea the trauma that awaits them if they get tangled up with anyone with those characteristics. The movie screen and real life are two different things. May we do our best to teach your youth to treat one another with mutual respect and remain sensitive to each other's feelings.

My dear friend, sister, and colleague, Rev. Dr. Stephanie Allen will share her insights, words of wisdom, and challenge on encouraging the values of equity and inclusion in the church and society.

* * * * * * * * * * * * * * *

Equity Is Deeper Than Optics

Rev. Dr. Stephanie Allen, D. Min, Senior Pastor, Memorial Baptist Church, Middlebury, Vermont

I have been drawn recently to the problem of spiritual immaturity in our churches, especially in our leadership. Seven out of the ten churches were brought up on charges in the book of Revelation of spiritual immaturity. We live in a world that is often satisfied with just looking grown-up. A world where there is a focus on the optics. If all the optics are achieved, we assume people have reached maturity. I have been in ministry for over twenty-six years. I have experienced the struggle with optics in being a woman, married to a brown man, and having interracial children. One of our daughters is from Guam. I have been heralded as a "savior" for adopting a brown child in a world that sees the optics of our situation. We have been heralded as saviors when we adopted two sons with special needs. And I have both been condemned for being a female pastor and bolstered for being a trailblazer. I am the first female pastor at the church I serve, which has been a challenge to navigate the bumpy terrain of looking past the optics. Optics can hide the heart of those struggling with the reality of living in a world that tends to judge the surface as having "arrived." The truth, however, of current-day ministry is that the focus on what the leader looks like instead of how a shepherd serves and leads has led to a burned-out flock of pastors.

There can be physical growth in the kingdom with no actual, systemic change. We can insert all the right players and none of the advancement of the ball down the field. We can add the extra seats at the table and not check to see if the chairs are quality. We settle then for the optics to determine one's fruit in ministry, and we seek to determine the invisible in a world that says a white male pastor is the ideal. I recently had a statement made by an applicant for a high-level ministerial position to me who said women were the second choice or plan B for God in ministry. If a pastor to other pastors can miss what is underneath our skin, then how can we discern leadership? First Samuel 16 is God's words to Samuel in directing his eyes to David as the next king.

> But the LORD said to Samuel, "Do not look on his appearance or on the height of his stature, because I have rejected him. For the LORD sees not as man sees: man looks on the outward appearance, but the LORD looks on the heart." (1 Samuel 16:7, ESV)

God judges the heart (*lev* in Hebrew), which is not an emotive place but the very center of our thoughts and being. He knows our hearts, minds, and very soul. I have also been struck by the qualifications for ministry as listed in the New Testament. Qualifications that were used against me as a woman because I didn't look the part. Qualifications such as "must be blameless—not overbearing, not quick-tempered, not given to drunkenness, not violent, not pursuing dishonest gain, one who loves what is good, who is self-controlled, upright, holy and disciplined" (Titus 7-8). If we hold those two verses up, the only one you could judge by appearance. It is almost as if God knew we would go for the things we can see and not seek the fruit born of righteousness.

I've been in ministry long enough to watch the pendulum swing to believe all women have a right to a seat at the table. I have seen a desire to try and be more inclusive in race. I have served a church that hired based on that inclusion. Both sound progressive. What I have also witnessed is that you can add a seat with no way of determining if it works or if it is even a viable seat at the table. We do this when support for women in ministry is more women-only groups for clergy. We allow for a seat, but often with no voice or leadership. My undergraduate work was in African American literature. A subject I naively thought I would teach one day, when God had other plans. The depth of raw vulnerability in an entire people group that is not truly being seen or heard in an integrated church is astounding. We often seek out the optics of a multicultural ministry, but not always with the intention of actually reflecting the kingdom.

What has happened in my own experience is then we want the optics and not the encounter with the person. We may want an integrated staff and not the fight for equality. We may want the female pastor but not the vantage point that comes with it. As a pastor, mother to eight children, a wife for twenty-five years who chooses to be poured out as a drink offering for the Lord. I do not want to be seen as having a right to ministry. I do not want to be seen externally at all, but rather the whole of me as I see the whole of you. I want to be righteous as I grow in spiritual maturity. To see the whole person includes their experience with the ways that ministry has hurt and limited as well as the freedom we see in Christ. Spiritual maturity is allowing the person to grow into who God called them to be. Our experiences with our gender and our race are part of that rich story. May I suggest that we do more than see each other in optics, but that we see each other in our experiences and that we listen to each other at the table. I suggest that we lean into the struggle each one of us faces together, not separate and isolated in groups that reflect the optics, and that we as the church speak into and trailblaze for holistic, kingdom-oriented ministry that helps us grow into spiritual maturity.

* * * * * * * * * * * * * * *

I am grateful for the voices of my friends! They highlight that women, young and old, from all cultures have experienced sexism, misogyny, and micro- and macro-aggressions. As shared in their testimonies and stories, Black and Brown women have the added struggles of intersectionality in both the church and secular realms. Their experiences are different than those of majority-culture women, particularly in the workplace. Organizational changes and strategies for creating healthier work environments are necessary to break the tide of pain and oppression.

Questions and Discussion Starters

Following are questions to help you contemplate, process, and share your thoughts.

1. Which one stood out to you the most from the testimonies shared? In what ways can you relate?
2. Have you seen or experienced sexism, racism, or other-isms in a work environment? Share an example.
3. What can individuals and groups do to influence churches and organizations to develop healthier work environments (mentally, physically, economically, etc.) for all people?
4. How can churches and other organizations help young people to embrace diversity, equity, and inclusion?
5. How would you advise someone who is experiencing any of the aforementioned experiences?

NOTES

1. Marin Hunter, "More Than a Ranking: Aris C. Smith" *Shakerite,* March 1, 2021, https://shakerite.com/?s=More+Than+a+Ranking.

2. Danielle Apugo, "A Hidden Culture of Coping: Insights on African American Women's Existence in Predominately White Institutions," *Multicultural Perspectives* 21, no. 1 (2019), 53–62, doi:10.1080/15210960.2019.1573067.

3. Christine A. Smith, "Lived Experiences of Inequity of African American Women Leading Struggling, Nonprofit Organizations in the United States: A Phenomenological Study," *Capella University*, 2022, ProQuest Dissertations Publishing. 28964693, 113.

4. Maura Cheeks, "How Black Women Describe Navigating Race and Gender in the Workplace," *Harvard Business Review,* March 26, 2018, https://hbr.org/2018/03/how-black-women-describe-navigating-race-and-gender-in-the-workplace.

5. Stephanie Pappas, "Effective therapy with Black women," *Monitor on Psychology* 52, no.8 (2021): 38, http://www.apa.org/monitor/2021/11/ce-therapy-black-women.

6. Emily Q. Ahonen, Kaori Fujishiro, Thomas Cunningham, and Michael Flinn, "Work as an inclusive part of population health inequities

research and prevention," *American Journal of Public Health* 108, no. 3, (2018): 306–11, https://doi.org/10.2105/AJPH.2017.304214.

7. Lauren Weber, "Inside Eli Lilly's Successful Strategy to Promote More Women," *Wall Street Journal,* October 15, 2019, https://www.wsj.com/articles/inside-eli-lillys-successful-strategy-to-promote-more-women-11571112180.

8. Smith, "Lived Experiences of Inequity of African American Women Leading Struggling, Nonprofit Organizations in the United States."

9. Marin Hunter, "More than a Ranking" *The Shakerite*, 2021, https://shakerite.com/campus-and-city/more-than-a-ranking/01/2021/.

CHAPTER 7

Poverty, Persuasion, and Power (Testimonies)

"I hate, I despise your religious festivals;
your assemblies are a stench to me.
Even though you bring me burnt offerings and grain offerings,
I will not accept them.
Though you bring choice fellowship offerings,
I will have no regard for them.
Away with the noise of your songs!
I will not listen to the music of your harps.
But let justice roll on like a river,
righteousness like a never-failing stream! —Amos 5:21-24

Political persuasion, power, and false piety converge to disenfranchise the impoverished. The testimonies from individuals who have been able to wake up from strategies used against them are both enlightening and instructive to hear.

In 2020, the COVID-19 pandemic descended upon us. The medical community, as well as the public, were mystified as this vicious disease ravaged individuals, families, businesses, and the world. Nobody at the time clearly understood the origins of the virus, how it spread, or the impact on our bodies. We had no idea of the havoc it would wreak upon our lives. People became impatient after months of uncertainty, and then resistance rose over the mandate that we had to wear masks to help prevent the spread. Schools shifted from in-person to virtual classes. The government forced businesses to close, some temporarily, some "until further notice." Hospitals and hospital workers at every level were traumatized, exasperated, and daunted. Funeral homes were overwhelmed by the number of bodies that were coming in. Hospitals restricted families from visiting their loved ones as they lay dying in the hospital hallways and on ventilators. It was a horrific season!

No community was impacted so severely as the homeless. The homeless, already relegated to the streets, under bridges, and being shuffled from shelter to shelter, suffered tremendously. In America, our safety net programs are broken. Those preaching "pro-life" are often the same ones who deny life-giving support to those most in need. On March 11, 2020, I shared the following reflection based on the scripture in the Old Testament book of Amos. Below is the reflection on my blog, *Shepastor*.[1]

Fasting From Injustice

This was a time of great wealth, economic growth, and national strength in Israel. The Northern and Southern Kingdoms (Israel and Judah) were working together trading, building, and forming political alliances. Because of their great wealth they were able to expand their borders. Their buildings were made of the finest materials, such as marble, ivory, and gold.

It was easy for them to equate their wealth and prosperity with the favor of God. Their prophets were in the pockets of those with power and prestige. Therefore, all of their proclamations pronounced favor, grace, and peace flowing from the throne of the Almighty.

But there was a problem in this man-made paradise. Contrary to what they believed, God was not pleased. There was a complete lack of social consciousness or concern. The wealthy were super wealthy, but the poor were super poor. The legal system was corrupt, the poor had no recourse, not even in the courts. The rich enjoyed every convenience possible while the poor were made to scrounge about and serve those in high positions—and God was not pleased.

There were no words of condemnation, confrontation, or accountability—and God was not pleased. Therefore, God called for himself a prophet—a real prophet, a man of God who neither desired their approval nor feared their reprisals. God chose Amos, who was neither a prophet nor the son of a prophet but a herdsman, a shepherd, a country boy if you will—a farmer to stand boldly and proclaim what thus saith the Lord to a wicked and sinful people. Amos spoke in righteous anger, calling God's people to look hard and long at what they had become.

We are currently in the season of the Christian calendar called "Lent." For many, this is a season of fasting from sweets and delectable goodies. The purpose is to sacrifice something that we enjoy in order to focus on getting closer to the Lord. The practice is admirable. Its intent is beautiful. But could the Lord be concerned about more than us giving up the chocolate bunnies, cakes, pies, etc.? It's easy to give up those things, but what does the Lord really want us to give up? What would truly be a "sacrifice"?

In Amos' day, people were fasting, attending religious gatherings, and even paying their tithes. But their hearts were far from the Lord. They were checking a proverbial box of religious behaviors. Today we must ask ourselves, "Are we any different?"

America is the wealthiest or at least one of the wealthiest nations on Earth. Yet in our land of plenty, there are millions of people living in poverty, homeless, hungry, and unable to meet their own basic needs. Poverty exists in every state across the country—in urban, suburban, and rural areas—and its reach crosses every barrier—age, race, gender, and family situation. Poverty can be situational (people experiencing a crisis such as illness, divorce, or unemployment), generational (families living in poverty for two or more generations), or relational (isolated people without a support network to turn to).

People in poverty experience not only a lack of income or material possessions but a lack of such things as life choices, physical and emotional security, stable relationships, social participation, and self-esteem. Poverty is teaching millions of Americans that they are not valued, that failure is to be expected, and that hope is futile.

Our approach to poverty has to change. Meeting immediate needs is wonderful, but if we don't challenge the systems that perpetuate poverty, our gifts are but Band-Aids on devastating wounds that require major surgery. We must fast from more than candy and other sweets; we need to fast from injustice! Crazy wealth for some and crazy poverty for many is unjust. We ought to have righteous anger, righteous indignation that shakes us from our spiritual lethargy and asks the question, "What can we do? What can I do to help make a difference?"

As the church, we need to begin to prayerfully ask God in 2020 what new things we can do to help bring about relief and support to our surrounding communities and the world. We need to ask ourselves the question, "Are we simply bringing before the Lord meaningless fasts, burnt offerings, and sacrifices of tradition and that which does not require us to leave our comfort zones?" How can we come together with other churches to collaborate to meet some needs right in our backyard? God desires more than us meeting together on Sunday morning to sing and pray. The Lord wants to use us to help break some chains, open some blinded eyes, bring some relief, to show his love and compassion to a dying world . . . to "do justice!"

Let us prayerfully consider what we can do to help serve this present age. As we fast and pray during this Lenten season, may our fasting cleanse us from lethargic and selfish ways. May our fasting convict us of empty practices. May our fasting pull us toward actions that give God's heart joy. May we fast from injustice!

A Change of Heart and Mind: A Former Racist Activist and a Rural, Young, White Male

In 2013, reporters from the Southern Poverty Law Center interviewed a young man who decided to abandon the white nationalist movement. The interview was with Derek Black, the son of Don Black, a former Alabama Klan leader.[2] At the time, Black was twenty-four years old. I find it interesting that his last name was Black. How challenging it must have been for him to carry that name along with his belief system.

Derek Black was raised as a racist and willingly participated in the movement. Being the son of a leading Klansman in Alabama, we can only imagine the level of influence surrounding an impressionable youth. He held to the propaganda and beliefs of his family, that the separation of the races was God-ordained and that white people were chosen by God to have dominion over all others. He held this belief until he went to college. There, after having met and ultimately become friends with students from varying backgrounds, particularly Jewish and Black, he began to question his belief system.

While he initially remained committed to his original thinking, he slowly began to realize that the people he loved, the men he admired, and the movement he followed were horribly flawed. In Derek Black's words, he began to disentangle himself from white nationalism. He acknowledged that his words and actions were "harmful to people of color, people of Jewish descent, activists striving for opportunity and fairness for all, and others affected."[3]

Derek Black then shared that advocating for "oppressed white people" in the West was damaging to all others because white privilege is something afforded to white people in all societies. Black stated, "Promoting a victim complex for whites does not recognize the oppressed experiences of others not in the position of a white person in society, and that's what my efforts have done."[4] Black's story was featured in Pulitzer Prize–winning journalist Eli Saslow's book *Rising Out of Hatred*.[5]

In Chapter 2, I referenced the documentary *Bad Faith*.[6] The movie highlighted the attempts of Christian nationalists to "Christianize America." Through this "Christian" rhetoric, many young white men, desiring to walk with Christ and spread the gospel, all while honoring their nation, were drawn to their movement. One young man in particular was Jonathan Wilson-Hartgrove, author of *Revolution of Values*. He shared that the "moral majority" believed that it was important for them to promote an ideology that they had the authority of God to advance a partisan agenda. They landed on the side of the Republican Party. They taught their listeners that the GOP was "God's party."[7]

Through the Council for Public Policy, major funding was provided to the Christian nationalist movement from oil companies. Pushing the pro-life agenda was paramount to this partnership. Born in poverty-stricken, rural North Carolina, "Tobacco Country," Wilson-Hartgrove shares that massive amounts of money were used to target communities like his—poor and white, struggling, yet religious, ripe for the picking. They were part of the master plan to build a coalition of white people from both rural areas and the suburbs who would become conservative voters.

Wilson-Hartgrove was drawn to the movement because he desired to serve Jesus and advance the pro-life causes, aligned with his faith.[8] He became involved in "formation programs" for youth designed by the religious right leaders. At the tender age of sixteen, Wilson-Hartgrove applied and was accepted as a page in the office of then-Senator Strom Thurmond.

Senator Thurmond was a well-known segregationist. He campaigned on racism and segregation and was successful for many years. The youth in the formation programs were encouraged to vote for people like Strom Thurmond because they were pro-life. But as Wilson-Hartgrove became more involved in Thurmond's campaigns and office, he quickly learned that the Senator had no true concerns for the life of the unborn. It was a ruse—something that was used to influence the unwitting, gain their votes, and perpetuate the money-making tactics of the movement. At the time, Senator Thurmond was the chair of the Senate Armed Services Committee, so his primary concern was to serve the interests of the military contractors.[9]

Wilson-Hartgrove shared, "I began to question whether biblical values really mattered much to these folks."[10] Feeling disillusioned and hoodwinked, he began to rethink his involvement with the religious right. He left Washington, DC, and returned home. Still interested in politics and making a positive impact for Christ, he attended a meeting hosted by the North Carolina Governor's Office. The guest speaker for the day was civil rights activist William Barber II. He, along with many other young people in attendance, was so inspired and challenged by Barber's message that he experienced a transformation. At the age of seventeen, Wilson-Hartgrove began being mentored by Barber. He became engaged in civil rights activism. He was drawn to civil rights because he saw the people who "took their faith very seriously, but always connected that with work for justice in the world."[11] Jonathan Wilson-Hartgrove's testimony is a prime example of how poverty, persuasion, and power converge to give the appearance of godliness, while the true motivation is greed.

Below is a word of testimony and challenge from my dear friend and colleague Dr. Judy K. Stewart. She cautions us about the lure and deceit of greed.

* * * * * * * * * * * * * * *

Greed Is Not Wealth

Judy K. Stewart, PhD, co-founder of the Virginia Science Technology Engineering and Applied Mathematics (STEAM) Academy—a multi-dimensional statewide initiative aimed at nurturing the next generation of STEAM leaders

"And behold a voice came to him and said, 'What are you doing here, Elijah?'" —1 Kings 19:13(b)

I don't watch the news like I used to. At one time, I was a self- (if not family-) diagnosed news junkie. But in late 2023, early 2024, I stepped away from all media and immersed myself in the Word of God. While I didn't stay away long, the respite helped me to consume news differently. I now intentionally seek the Holy Spirit's guidance in truth, self-awareness, and courage when I read or listen to the news.

The prophet Elijah offers a profile in discernment and courage. In 1 Kings 18, we witness a showdown at Mount Carmel. Elijah confronts the Israelites who have been deceived into fearing and following wicked King Ahab. "Elijah asks the people, 'How long will you waver between two opinions? If the Lord is God, follow Him; but if Baal is God, follow him.' But the people said nothing" (1 Kings 18:21). The scriptures record that Elijah challenges Baal's prophets to a contest. They agree to chop two bulls in pieces and put them on wood. Whichever god answers with fire will be declared the true god.

With the rules defined, Elijah invites Baal's prophets to go first. He teases them when there is no answer from Baal. Perhaps your god is sleeping, he says. Shout a little louder. Exhausted and demoralized, Baal's prophets finally give up. Elijah repairs the Lord's altar. He orders a handful of Israelites to participate in the expected miracle by saturating the sacrifice and wooden altar with water three times. Then, he prays to God. Not only does God consume the sacrifice, but he burns up the wood, the stones, the soil, and all the water in the surrounding trench. The people fall on their faces and declare, "The Lord—He is God! The Lord—He is God!" (v. 39). Riding high, Elijah orders the prophets of Baal to be executed. But then King Ahab's wife, Jezebel, delivers a threatening message to Elijah: What you did to my prophets, I will do to you. This one message sends Elijah fleeing into the wilderness, where he eventually hides in a cave. After forty days, he hears from God in a gentle whisper, "Elijah, what are you doing here?"

Perhaps the church is a modern-day Elijah. How long will we waver between two opinions? How long will we juxtapose our carnal greed, for example, with our kingdom call to serve, honor, and help the least among us? How long will we rationalize our $38 billion selfish, self-storage industry against the needs of the unhoused (600,000 and counting in 2023, according to the US Department of Housing and Urban Development)? How long will we wink and nod at the hyper-gentrification of neighborhoods at the expense of affordable housing for poor and working-class people?

I caught a story on the CBS Evening News' *Eye on America* segment this summer in which a firefighter/paramedic, along with his wife and young daughter, shared that he cannot afford to live in Jackson, Wyoming, where he grew up and still serves. Jackson Hole has become a vacation spot for the uber-rich. The average price for a single-family home is $7.4 million. "I'm the help, even though I'm a firefighter/paramedic," he said. "Once we're done doing the job, we're expected to kick rocks, get lost."

Greed is not wealth. The Oxford Dictionary defines *greed* as "intense and selfish desire for something, especially wealth, power, or food." Greed is the exaltation of something. It is often accompanied, particularly in the case of wealth and power, by arrogance and feigned, paltry care (or utter disregard) for others. Greed and its foul first cousins lead us away from our core directive to love God and to love one another. A telling scripture in the

Old Testament warns against greed. In Hosea, God says, "When I fed them, they were satisfied; when they were satisfied, they became proud; then they forgot Me" (Hosea 13:6).

> *Greed demands more.* But his Word says, "[m]y God shall supply all your need according to His riches in glory by Christ Jesus." —Philippians 4:19
>
> *Greed declares, "This is mine."* But his Word says, "The earth is the Lord's, and all it contains. The world, and those who live in it." —Psalm 24:1
>
> *Greed elevates our wants.* But his Word says, "The Lord is my shepherd. I shall not want." —Psalm 23:1
>
> *Greed cannot be satisfied.* But his Word says, "I have learned the secret of being content in any and every situation, whether well fed or hungry, whether living in plenty or in want. I can do all things through Him who gives me strength." —Philippians 4:12-13

As the body of Christ, I wonder if our sacrifice is fully saturated. I wonder if we have had enough of our greed and economic injustice. I wonder if we have the courage to call on the Lord in prayer and the self-awareness to seek him in truth. Perhaps God will find us in the same position as Elijah and ask, "Have I not performed a Mount Carmel in your life? Have I not healed you, restored you, given you grace beyond measure? Then how is it that you, who know me to be your God, can be found trembling with fear, hiding from this day's challenge?"

People of God, what are we doing here?

* * * * * * * * * * * * * * *

The convergence of poverty, political persuasion, and power is real! Again, my friends helped us to reflect upon the impact of false piety and politics in the lives of the impoverished, including poor white people. We owe a debt of gratitude to those who have transparently shared (as in the *Bad Faith* documentary reviewed in this chapter) what it meant to wake up from the strategies used against them to advance hatred, injustice, and racism disguised as Christianity.

Questions and Discussion Starters

Below are questions do help you contemplate, process, and share your thoughts.

1. In what ways do false piety, poverty, and power continue to impact American society today?
2. In your opinion, how have poverty, political persuasion, and power converged to blind people, blocking them from seeing "the man behind the curtain"?
3. Do you have family members, friends, or acquaintances who hold political beliefs that are polar opposite from yours? If so, how have your differences impacted your relationship(s)?
4. How can churches and other organizations help to bring people together, even when they have differing ideologies?
5. In your opinion, should we have these discussions within the context of the church? Why or why not?

NOTES

1. Christine A. Smith, "Fasting From Injustice," *Shepastor,* March 11, 2020, https://shepastor.blogspot.com/2020/03/shepastor-fasting-from-injustice.html.

2. Mark Potok and Laurie Wood, "Leaving White Nationalism," *Southern Poverty Law Center,* August 2013, Fall Issue, https://www.splcenter.org/fighting-hate/intelligence-report/2013/leaving-white-nationalism.

3. Potok and Wood, "Leaving White Nationalism."

4. Potok and Wood, "Leaving White Nationalism."

5. Terry Gross, "How a Rising Star of white Nationalism Broke Free from the Movement," *NPR,* September 24, 2018, https://www.npr.org/2018/09/24/651052970/how-a-rising-star-of-white-nationalism-broke-free-from-the-movement.

6. Stephen Ujlaki, Co-Director, Christopher Jones, *Bad Faith: Christian Nationalism's Unholy War on Democracy*, San Francisco: The Film Sales Company, 2024, https://www.badfaithdocumentary.com/about.
7. Ujlaki, *Bad Faith.*
8. Ujlaki, *Bad Faith.*
9. Ujlaki, *Bad Faith.*
10. Ujlaki, *Bad Faith.*
11. Ujlaki, *Bad Faith.*

CHAPTER 8

What Then Shall We Do? Being the Change

To enact change, practical strategies to recognize, address, and disrupt, sexist, racist, and poverty-inducing structures are necessary. Sometimes we benefit from examples and find inspiration in the stories of others living into their calls. My doctoral mentor and friend, Dr. Jolee Darnell, shares insights, words of wisdom, and challenges concerning *being the change*.

* * * * * * * * * * * * * * *

Embodying Change

Jolee Darnell, PhD, MSW, Part-Time Faculty, School of Public Service and Education, Capella University

There is an often-quoted statement reflecting on the perspective that evil will triumph over good if good people stand by and do not act. The quote is, "Bad men need nothing more to compass their ends, than that good men should look on and do nothing." This quote is attributed to an address by John Stuart Mill at the 1867 University of St. Andrews inaugural address.[1] This perspective about acting relates that there is a complacency of belief that, if we do not take a position or form an opinion, we can allow or even facilitate negative beliefs and behaviors. John Mill championed a position most specifically about how social design and beliefs have sometimes blatantly and sometimes subtly facilitated injustice and a demeanor that one group has power or dominion over another group.[2]

In any consideration about being a change in our world, we all bring some of our own world perspectives to the issues we choose to champion. Having spent time as a female service member in a male-dominated military world and as a white woman in a community that was diverse in both religious and racial composition, I have been in situations that pushed me to look at many life situations through views other than those that were developed from my own life experiences.

In every diverse community experience, there are those who take pride in uplifting their community and those who choose to be bystanders in the events occurring around them.

The pride of *brotherhood* is a significant aspect of the military community. Perspectives of "we look out for our own" are prevalent in military culture. However, when looking at the nature of change in this close-knit culture, a female parent service member often continues to live at or below the poverty line and often still needs to apply for housing and food assistance.[3] Even in the changing culture of the military, only about 18 percent of the Armed Forces demographic is female,[4] compared to about 50 percent female population in the US collectively. Breaking down gender-aligned barriers is a part of the cultural change that needs to occur collectively. Those of us who have been part of creating this change need to encourage others to follow in our footsteps (or boot steps, as the case may be).

The military is, in some ways, presented as a great financial opportunity equalizer, as both male and female service members receive the same pay for the same rank, so financial equity issues are less obvious, except when it comes to promotions and opportunities to excel. Female career opportunities are often limited or still more prevalent in some job categories such as the medical field. There is still a focus on military parents that favors the career of the male military member over the female military member. How do we as a system overtly or covertly allow or encourage these courses of action?

Political and social change for gender roles only comes when voices are raised to facilitate more active integration. There are some indications that such integration has a more positive impact on the fears of the potential negative impacts that come with upholding the status quo.[5] Certainly, fear of change is a significant factor in resistance to change. Yet in my own military life experience, I saw many women leaders who were both tough and fair. Often, I heard the message from some of my female colleagues that there is a compassionate side to leadership, and that women leaders demonstrated their capacity to administer consequences as well as promote personal and professional development.

In 2020, the Brookings Institution published a gender equality series about the integration and diversification of the American Armed Forces.[6] The study had some relevant and timely recommendations for actions that can and should be taken—and here is that edict again—in order for change to occur, action must be taken. There is a recommendation to create a wider recruitment pool—to look in areas for recruitment and engagement that may typically be overlooked, and to help facilitate an honor code to serve one's country. In our political social structure today, there are more women serving in political leadership positions who have served in military leadership positions. The lead-by-example practice is so important to the ability to facilitate change in the world.

We are living amid a culture in which those who do not share the perspectives espoused by the loudest voices often seem to be reticent to speak up in contrast and call out false, demeaning, and destructive attitudes, behaviors, and perspectives. How do we give voice to the more compassionate perspectives in the face of those who seem to believe it is acceptable to use insulting and demeaning language to shut down alternative viewpoints?

As we move toward more equality in practice, there are some perspectives to consider about our own engagement, including the call to have our practices demonstrate our commitment to change and the call to make use of our talents. These are both practical and biblical perspectives. The admonitions that reflect we will be known by the fruits that we bear (Matthew 7:15-20) and the call to use our talents wisely (Matthew 25:14-30) are both powerful messages about our call to action. Wherever we are in our lives, in small communities, in diverse cultures, or in specialized communities, being the change that others see is our call to action.

* * * * * * * * * * * * * * *

I am grateful to my doctoral studies mentor, Jolee Darnell, for sharing her insights as a woman veteran. Her practical strategies to recognize, address, and disrupt sexist, racist, and poverty-inducing structures within the United States military system are important for us to receive and understand. Her insights provide important guidance on ways to advocate for healthy changes for US service people.

Questions and Discussion Starters

Below are questions to help you contemplate, process, and share your thoughts.

1. What are some challenges that women in the military face? How might their experiences differ from those of males?
2. In your opinion, why do people choose to remain silent when they have opportunities to speak up against evil?
3. Share a time when either you spoke up or chose to remain silent. What would you do differently, if anything?
4. How can churches and other organizations encourage and empower individuals to become disrupters of sexist, racist, and poverty-inducing structures?
5. List the challenges associated with speaking up. How can you overcome these challenges?

NOTES

1. Susan Ratcliffe, *Oxford Essential Quotations, 5th ed.*, Oxford University Press, 2017.
2. Christopher Macleod, "John Stuart Mill," *Stanford Encyclopedia of Philosophy*, https://plato.stanford.edu/archives/sum2020/entries/mill/.

3. Doug Irving, "Essay: Why are US Military Families Experiencing Food Insecurity?" *RAND Corporation,* https://www.rand.org/pubs/articles/2023/why-are-us-military-families-experiencing-food-insecurity.html.

4. US Department of Defense, "Department of Defense releases annual demographic report – Upward trend in number of women serving continues," https://www.defense.gov/News/Releases/Release/Article/3246268/department-of-defense-releases-annual-demographics-report-upward-trend-in-numbe/.

5. João Carlos Gonçalves dos Reis and Sofia Menezes, "Gender Inequalities in the Military Service: A Systematic Literature Review," *Sexuality & Culture,* June, 2020, DOI:10.1007/s12119-019-09662-y.

6. Lori Robinson and Michael E. O'Hanlon, "Women Warriors: The Ongoing Story of Integrating and Diversifying the Armed Forces," *Brookings Institution,* 2020, https://www.brookings.edu/articles/women-warriors-the-ongoing-story-of-integrating-and-diversifying-the-armed-forces/.

CHAPTER 9

A Final Word for Churches, Secular Organizations, and Community Leaders

I was inspired to write *Deconstructing Power and Isms within the Church and Society* because of the devastating ways the Christian religion is being used to oppress, disenfranchise, and make rich specific groups of people. The tactics used by the greedy are not new. Those who use the methods discussed brush off, shine up, and repurpose their strategies. As God's word declares, "There is nothing new under the sun" (Ecclesiastes 1:9).

I owe a debt of gratitude to my mentors, friends, and colleagues for taking time out of their busy schedules to join me in this project. Our prayer is that the words therein will provide enlightenment, challenge, contemplation, and a call to action. So what did we learn as a church and society?

False Piety and Power Revisited

Early in this book, we read several examples of how false piety and power have worked for hundreds of years in America. As our nation teeters on the brink of a broken democratic system, it is critical to understand these truths about our history as a nation. We remembered how just when Americans believed we had turned the proverbial corner on racism after electing our first Black president, Barack Obama, a tsunami of white backlash descended upon us. White and Christian nationalism rampantly spread with the election of Donald J. Trump. We cannot overestimate the negative impact of hate speech, otherisms, and right-wing politics upon women, Black and Brown people, and the poor.

We also examined bad theology and power structures, reflecting on Jesus' prayer for his disciples as he prepared to make the ultimate sacrifice for humanity. Jesus reminded his followers that they are *in the world* but not *of the world.* The distinction between those two realities was laid bare by reviewing Jesus' ministry, false piety, and how those concepts play out in today's culture. We have witnessed how the misinterpretation of the scriptures has been systemically used to advance patriarchy, racism, sexism, and the oppression of specific groups of people.

We explored common barriers that women and people of color face and the concept of the glass cliff. False piety, patriarchal structures, and barriers to advancement opportunities for women, Black and Brown people continuously interplay with each other to reinforce glass ceilings and cliffs. What do we have yet to discover when it comes to dismantling barriers? We know that Black and Brown women are underrepresented in lead/executive-level positions in both religious and secular realms. We also know that when they do gain access, they are frequently appointed to glass cliff positions/organizations. We know that they are daunted by unrealistic expectations and stereotypes that stakeholders use to determine the level of their effectiveness.

We also know that a deliberate erasure of history concerning the treatment of people of color in America has stymied the dismantling of racism in our nation. What we lack is substantial information about the lived experiences of oppressed people upon their beings, in their own words. We have read many reasons why their voices and insights are necessary for the breaking of unjust and inequitable structures. What more do we need to learn before we take action to overcome the problems of this world?

Becoming Not of This World

Renaissance literary genius the late Zora Neale Hurston shared that her mother encouraged her to "jump at de sun," explaining that you may not reach the sun, but at least you will get off the ground.[1] We have worked to deconstruct the realities of politics and power. The work can seem daunting; however, hope should never be lost. We too should take hold of Zora's mother's words of wisdom. We must continue to press forward to rise higher and strive to dismantle systems of oppression in America. Hearing from others working to overcome these issues is inspiring, and we have read several of my friends, colleagues, and mentors' insights, words of wisdom, challenges, and counsel from their own experiences. My dear mentor and friend, James C. Perkins encouraged us with words of wisdom, insight, and challenge, invoking the Civil Rights Movement mantra, "We shall overcome!"

Let's break it down: we focused on the politics of the powerful, zeroing in on the tactics of the beneficiaries of colonialism, and the proponents of racist sexist power structures. Examples of how oppressed people are conditioned to perpetuate their oppression were given. We explored how sexism, racism, and glass cliffs function systemically in America. Intersectionality was discussed and exemplified through testimonies/anecdotes of majority culture persons, and Black and Brown women in both the church and secular realms.

We unpacked the convergence of poverty, false piety, political persuasion, and power in America. The discussion included testimonies from a former white nationalist and a former Christian nationalist on how they woke up to break free from the deceptive, destructive, and dangerous movements. After all the things we considered, we were challenged to ask ourselves, "What then shall we do?" My doctoral mentor, Jolee Darnell, offers words from the perspective of a white woman who served in the military, emphasizing the importance of speaking up and being the change we hope to see. She offered practical strategies to recognize, address, and disrupt sexist, racist, and poverty-inducing structures within specific contexts given.

Dismantling Abusive Power and Isms in the Church and Society Is Possible: A Concluding Message

Arguably, the twentieth century (1901–2000) was remarkable, filled with events that changed the inner workings of America. Some of the most consequential pieces of legislation were passed that expanded the middle class and broke the back of abhorrent racist and sexist policies. Once these freedoms were gained, however, many were seemingly lulled asleep. Warranted is a brief review of the historic measures that truly made America great to some degree.

One Step Forward, Many Steps Backward

Following the Civil War, the nation grappled with its new identity. The end of slavery briefly opened the door for a new path. Fresh winds began to blow as Black men were recognized as intelligent human beings capable of participating in the leadership of our nation as members of Congress (Reconstruction era).[2]

Unfortunately, this newfound freedom was short-lived. Soon, the ghosts of the former era arose, dragging our nation backward to the establishment of Jim Crow laws. From 1865–1965, America reneged on its promises and opportunities for Black people to breathe free and live as citizens. Jim Crow laws canceled the rights of Black men to vote (women's right to vote had not yet been instituted). These laws also denied Black people the rights of employment, education, integration with white people, and intermarriage.[3] It took one hundred years to undo President Rutherford B. Hayes' Compromise of 1877 (an informal agreement between supporters and Hayes and Southern Democrats to settle the 1876 presidential election), ending Reconstruction, removing federal troops from Southern states, and abandoning free Black people to the whims and wishes of racist white people.[4]

FDR's New Deal Era and the Expansion of the Middle Class

Although it would take approximately three more decades before more equitable policies for Black, Brown, and poor people came about, the 1930s ushered in a president who was a groundbreaking leader—one who paved the way for all Americans to have a shot at the American dream.

President Franklin Delano Roosevelt (1933–1945) entered the White House near the decade-long Great Depression (1929–1941). This "New Deal" president laid the groundwork for the many social service programs in our nation today.[5] Roosevelt was determined to change the tide of America's cataclysmic economic failure to major economic growth for Americans. From the beginning of his four terms, Roosevelt dedicated his presidential endeavors to lifting Americans out of poverty and undergirding their potential for financial stability. He restored trust in the banking system by establishing the Federal Deposit Insurance Corporation (FDIC), which insures individual bank accounts.[6]

Roosevelt also addressed high levels of unemployment by establishing the Works Progress Administration (WPA) and the Civilian Conservation Corps (CCC), programs that provided emergency and short-term government aid through job opportunities. Temporary employment was provided through construction projects and work on national forests.[7] One of FDR's most notable accomplishments was the establishment of the Social Security Board (SSB), which provides (to this day) benefits to older Americans, widows, unemployment compensation, and disability insurance. Protections such as maximum working hours, minimum wage, child labor laws, and a variety of regulatory practices all helped to strengthen the middle class.[8] Roosevelt's policies also provided additional impetus for disenfranchised people to fight for their rights.

Civil Rights

Brave women and men of many hues and faith traditions—white, Black, Brown, Jews, Christians, Muslims, etc., banded together to fight for the civil rights of all. On August 6, 1965, with Martin Luther King Jr. and others standing over his shoulder, President Lyndon Baines Johnson signed the Voting Rights Act. With the stroke of a pen, the discriminatory practices of literacy tests and legacy voting (for example, ownership of land, grandfather's right to vote necessary for the next generation to have the right to vote, etc.) were outlawed. One hundred years after the end of Reconstruction, these rights were finally restored.

I have briefly described endeavors of the immediate past century to emphasize that many of these benefits and freedoms are on proverbial life support in the twenty-first century. Below is a list of bills passed that shaped the twentieth century in America.[9] Each of these bills moved our nation forward, addressed our health and well-being, strengthened the middle class, and tackled issues of inequity:

Federal-Aid Highway Act–1956
National Defense Education Act–1958
Civil Rights Act–1964
Voting Rights Act–1965
Amendments to Immigration and Nationality Act–1965
Medicare and Medicaid Acts–1965
Clean Air Act Amendments–1970
Comprehensive Drug Abuse Prevention and Control Act–1970
Amendments to the Social Security Act–1972
End of military draft–1973
Economic Recovery Tax Act–1981

Gun-Free School Zones Act–1990
The Brady Handgun Violence Prevention Act–1993[10]

Will It Take Another Hundred Years to Get Back on Track?

The list above provides a glimpse of the major ways in which Americans came together to expand wealth opportunities for all. Certainly, not all legislation passed in the twentieth century promoted equity, but significant pieces of legislation did. Civil rights, voting rights, rights for immigrants, rights for the elderly, help for our educational systems, concern over our environment, and gun control were all issues that influenced legislators to work together and send bills to the desks of both Democratic and Republican presidents. Taken together, all these endeavors gave our nation at least a shot at a more perfect union.

During former President Biden's farewell speech on Wednesday, January 17, 2025, prophetically, he boldly warned America about what was at stake. Biden not only discussed legislation passed during his administration that is in the vein of helping all Americans to rise, but he also talked about how we have entered a perilous season. He warned that we are leaving the era of middle-class expansion and rapidly returning to an era when oligarchs (the extremely wealthy) controlled how our nation works. Biden stated:

> Today an oligarchy is taking shape in America of extreme wealth and influence that literally threatens our entire democracy, our basic rights and freedoms, and a fair shot for everyone to get ahead . . . Americans stood up to the robber barons. They didn't punish the wealthy, just made the wealthy play by the rules . . . The truth is smothered by lies told for power and for profit . . . Americans are being buried under an avalanche of misinformation

> and disinformation enabling abuse of power. The free press is crumbling, others are disappearing, and social media has given up on fact-checking.[11]

Elon Musk, Mark Zuckerberg, Scott Bezos, Donald Trump, and others are escalating the use of wealth to threaten the freedom of the Press, strong-arm or buy news organizations, spin lies that create public distrust of legitimate news, undermine trust in established medical protocols (such as vaccines), etc. Biden encouraged the nation to remember the real greatness of America—that we are a nation that rose above our differences to come together and do amazing things. Democracy is in our hands. It is teetering, but we can restore stabilization. The question is whether we have the courage, wisdom, will, and humility to learn from our past and turn to a bright, hopeful future.

False piety and the abuse of power were present in biblical times and today, in both the church and society. We can turn a blind eye and stick our proverbial heads in the sand or speak up and become engaged. We can study the issues, learn from one another, and vote in ways that advance equity, opportunity, mercy, and justice.

A Path Forward

Throughout this book, we have explored the foundations of our America as well as ways in which the church and society have engaged in abuses of power and oppression of specific groups of people. At the root of our struggle is coming to grips with attitudes and actions that have harmed human beings. While it takes courage to stand up and speak truth to power, it also takes humility to look in the proverbial mirror and ask ourselves, "Are my actions and attitudes toward others based upon justice, mercy, and humility? How would I feel if someone were treating me the way that I am treating them? Have I used my power to help or hurt others? Am

I willing to look at life through the eyes of other people?" Finally, "Am I willing to do what is necessary to change and influence change for the better?"

The church teaches the importance of forgiveness and, when possible, reconciliation. Forgiveness is a personal decision to reject acts of vengeance, carrying a grudge, dwelling upon unjust and painful experiences of the past (and sometimes current), and hatred. Forgiveness does not require a change in the perpetrator. It does not hold as a prerequisite the perpetrator's repentance, request for forgiveness, or acknowledgment of wrong. Forgiveness requires the victim to reject a vengeful spirit in exchange for healing, self-care, mercy, and love. It requires embracing the counterintuitive instruction of Jesus to turn the other cheek and pray for our enemies. Forgiveness calls us to live out love's mandate and take the more excellent way.

Reconciliation is something altogether different. Reconciliation cannot occur with just one. It requires a mutual agreement between two or more people that someone or something was harmed. It requires acknowledgment of wrong, lament over wrongs committed, repentance, restoration, and change. Christlike love and the precious Holy Spirit enable the people of God to embrace forgiveness. Sadly, much less is taught concerning the process of reconciliation. Society teaches the importance of forgiveness in both sacred and secular realms. Therapeutic processes regarding the benefits of forgiveness for victims are widespread in psychology, psychiatry, theology, etc. Reconciliation, however, is most often unpacked in the arena of social justice.

The late Archbishop Desmond Tutu, a South African Anglican priest, provided a transformational model of reconciliation as he led the Truth and Reconciliation Commission (TRC).[12] In 1995, the South African Parliament, under the leadership of the late President Nelson Mandela (activist/politician who vigorously stood against the South African apartheid system, led the resistance movement to change it, and became South Africa's first democratically elected president in 1994) authorized the formation of the TRC.[13] The TRC was formed to enable reconciliation and forgiveness among the victims of apartheid and its leaders/participants.

The TRC allowed victims of the apartheid atrocities to express their pain, rage, and bewilderment. The proceedings also allowed victims to hear the full disclosure of the truth. Through the TRC, the apartheid regime was found guilty of gross human rights violations. The process also opened the door for paying reparations to victims and their families, as well as amnesty to those who fully disclosed their participation in the violence.[14]

Led by Tutu, the Truth and Reconciliation Commission was pivotal in showing the world that forgiveness and reconciliation are possible even after the most horrific acts have been committed. It was not easy, but it was possible. A path forward was carved because participants could speak truthfully, and there was an acknowledgment of wrong, admission to participation in the wrong, hearts of lament, and a determination to restore. Absent these components, calling people to become reconciled is hollow. We *can* choose the path forward, but will we?

The persons who initially robbed Indigenous people of their land and forced them onto reservations are now long dead. The slave owners who violently captured and enslaved Black people from the continent of Africa are now long dead. The systems that were created to perpetuate their oppression are still very much alive. Americans may not be able to hold truth and reconciliation hearings in the same sense exhibited by South Africa, but we can take from their example and apply aspects of their methods to our efforts to heal our land.

Instead of banning books and engaging in history erasure, people of faith, organizational leaders, educators, etc., can be intentional about helping others to learn the foundations of the abuses of power and isms in America. We can confront false piety by being an example of God's true love. We can host community dialogues surrounding issues of injustice. We can teach our children to get to know people for themselves instead of believing stereotypes. We can participate in strategic planning to address societal inequities. We can hold government leaders accountable by learning their platforms, examining their voting records, and voting them out of office if their actions contribute to systemic oppression. These are just a few examples of how we can move ahead in positive ways.

About seven years ago, one of the three major health systems in Cleveland invited community members to a series of meetings to discuss health disparities between white people and minorities, the economically depressed, and those who have means in the surrounding community. Our local clergy group was included in the discussions. The group I worked with was asked to make a list of what we perceived to be social determinants of health outcomes in the area. The lack of mainline grocery stores in poor neighborhoods was uppermost on the minds of many. Pastors (including myself) shared how some church members had to take three buses to go to a grocery store. One can imagine what it was like for them to have to walk to the bus stop, change buses several times, do the actual grocery shopping, and then turn around, carry their groceries back to the bus stop, onto the buses, and then walk home.

The stores that once stood in the community were shuttered or occupied by grocers who carried subpar food at high prices. During our discussion, some people began exploring the ideas of community gardens and food trucks. However, several of us expressed frustration over those ideas. I specifically asked for a show of hands of how many of us rely on community gardens and food trucks to get our groceries. Not a hand went up.

We challenged the hospital (an extraordinarily wealthy conglomerate) to invest in the surrounding community by helping to bring one or two mainline grocery stores to the area. To God be the glory, our monthly sessions influenced change. A few years later, we saw two beautiful mainline grocery stores go up within some of the most economically depressed areas. I saw one of the stores featured on the news recently. It was that store's one-year anniversary. Members of the community were both shoppers and employees. Shoppers expressed their deep appreciation for the chance to buy fresh food at reasonable prices, have a large selection, and, most importantly, have all this available within walking distance of their homes.

Dialogue, pressure, and strategy helped to make a difference for the community. The church and society came together to help address a system that created health disparities in an impoverished area. Speaking up, showing up, and standing up moved the hospital from a conversation to an action. They used their dollars, relationships, and influence to bring healthy food options to the area. Our voices matter. Our actions matter even more. Freedoms and rights lost are never easily restored. We must use *our* money, relationships, and influence to restore, keep, and expand our rights and the rights of all.

It is never easy to stand up for what is just, merciful, and Christ-like love. John Oxenham put it like this,

> ***The Ways***
>
> *"To every man there openeth*
> *A way, and ways, and a way.*
> *And the high soul climbs the high way,*
> *And the low soul gropes the low:*
> *And in between, on the misty flats,*
> *The rest drift to and fro.*
> *But to every man there openeth*
> *A high way and a low,*
> *And every man decideth*
> *The way his soul shall go"*[15]

Jesus put it like this,

> Mark 8:34-36, KJV
> And when he had called the people unto him with his disciples also, he said unto them, Whosoever will come after me, let him deny himself, and take up his cross, and follow me.
> For whosoever will save his life shall lose it; but whosoever shall lose his life for my sake and the gospel's, the same shall save it.
> For what shall it profit a man, if he shall gain the whole world, and lose his own soul?
> Or what shall a man give in exchange for his soul?
>
> John 16:33
> "I have told you these things, so that in me you may have peace. In this world you will have trouble. But take heart! I have overcome the world."

Brenda Salter McNeill quotes Mark DeYmaz in *Roadmap to Reconciliation* who says, "Lament, repentance, reconciliation, and justice are not peripheral to the gospel but intrinsic to it."[16]

May we in the church and society lament, repent, reconcile, and be just. Then, we will find the path forward. May it not take another one hundred years.

Questions and Discussion Starters

Below are questions to help you contemplate, process, and share your thoughts.

1. In your opinion, which chapter was the most impactful for you? Why?
2. What in the book surprised you and why?

3. After reading this book, did anything change or impact your perspective on false piety and power?
4. How can churches and other organizations help to bring people together, even when they have differing ideologies?
5. In your opinion, should we have these discussions within the context of the church? Why or why not?

NOTES

1. Anthony Peyton Porter, "Jump at de Sun: The Story of Zora Neale Hurston," *Carolrhoda Books,* 1992, https://www.adl.org/jump-de-sun-story-zora-neale-hurston.

2. Zinn Education Project, "Oct 19, 1870: First African Americans Elected to the House of Representatives," n.d., https://www.zinnedproject.org/news/tdih/african-americans-house-of-reps/#:~:text=On%20Oct.,Rainey%2C%20Robert%20C.

3. Jim Crow Museum, "Compromise of 1877: The End of Reconstruction," *History*, November 27, 2019, https://www.history.com/topics/us-presidents/compromise-of-1877.

4. History.com Editors, "Compromise of 1877: The End of Reconstruction," History, November 27, 2019, https://www.history.com/topics/us-presidents/compromise-of-1877.

5. Catherine A. Paul, "The New Deal," in "Eras in Social Welfare: History, Great Depression," *Virginia Commonwealth University,* n.d., https://socialwelfare.library.vcu.edu/eras/great-depression/the-new-deal/.

6. Federal Reserve History, "Great Depression," *Federal Reserve History,* n.d., https://www.federalreservehistory.org/time-period/great-depression.

7. Paul, "The New Deal."

8. Paul, "The New Deal."

9. Louis Jacobson, "Ten Bills that Really Mattered," *Roll Call,* May 2, 2005, https://rollcall.com/2005/05/02/ten-bills-that-really-mattered/.

10. Chip Brownlee, "How 30 Years of Federal Background Checks Changed Gun Buying, by the Numbers," *The Trace: Investigating gun violence in America,* November 30, 2022. https://www.thetrace.org/2023/11/background-checks-gun-purchasing-brady/.

11. Brian Bennett, "Biden Says Goodbye-With Some Warnings," *Time,* January 16, 2025, https://www.aol.com/biden-says-goodbye-warnings-031359031.html.

12. Apartheid Museum, "The Truth and Reconciliation Commission," *TRC,* n.d., https://www.apartheidmuseum.org/exhibitions/the-truth-and-reconciliation-commission-trc#:~:text=In%20July%201995%20South%20Africa's,politically%20motivated%20human%20rights%20violations.

13. Nelson Mandela Foundation, "Biography of Nelson Mandela," *The Archive at the Centre of Memory*, n.d., https://www.nelsonmandela.org/biography.

14. The Editors of Encyclopedia Britannica, "Desmond Tutu," *Britannica*, December 22, 2024, https://www.britannica.com/biography/Desmond-Tutu.

15. Allpoetry.com, "The Ways by John Oxenham," *Allpoetry.com*, 2024, https://allpoetry.com/The-Ways.

16. Brenda Salter McNeil, *Roadmap to Reconciliation: Moving Communities into Unity, Wholeness, and Justice* (Downers Grove, IL: InterVarsity Press, 2015), 33.

Glossary of Terms

Agape: In scripture, the transcendent *agape* love is the highest form of love and is contrasted with *eros*, or erotic love, and *philia*, or brotherly love. ("Agape | Definition, Scripture, & Uses" 2023). "Agape | Definition, Scripture, & Uses," Encyclopedia Britannica, 2023, https://www.britannica.com/topic/agape.

Barrier: Anything that blocks or is intended to impede passage into or through a channel. For example, gender and race can intersect to form barriers to career ascension for Black women (Gamble & Turner, 2015; Salvaj & Kuschel, 2020). (Gamble, Erica D., and Norma J. Turner. "Career ascension of African American women in executive positions in post-secondary institutions." *Journal of Organizational Culture, Communications and Conflict* 19, no. 1 (2015): 82).

(Salvaj, Erica, and Katherina Kuschel. "Opening the "Black Box": Factors affecting women's journey to senior management positions—A literature review." *The new ideal worker: Organizations between work-life balance, gender and leadership* (2020): 203–222).

Deconstruct: To take apart or examine (something) in order to reveal the basis or composition often with the intention of exposing biases, flaws, or inconsistencies. "Definition of DECONSTRUCT," (n.d. www.merriam-webster.com), https://www.merriam-webster.com/dictionary/deconstruct.

Ecclesiastical: of or relating to a church especially as an established institution. "Definition of ECCLESIASTICAL," (n.d. Www.merriam-Webster.com), https://www.merriam-webster.com/dictionary/ecclesiastical.

Equality: (a) of the same measure, quantity, amount, or number as another; (c) not showing variation in appearance, structure, or proportion, "Definition of EQUAL," (Merriam-Webster.com, 2019), https://www.merriam-webster.com/dictionary/equal.

Equity: Justice according to natural law or right *specifically*: freedom from bias or favoritism, "Definition of EQUITY" (Merriam-Webster.com, 2019), https://www.merriam-webster.com/dictionary/equity.

Glass cliff: A phenomenon describing the reality that women are more likely than men to be appointed to precarious leadership positions in unstable, dysfunctional organizations (Morgenroth et al., 2020; Ryan et al., 2015).

(Morgenroth, Thekla, Teri A. Kirby, Michelle K. Ryan, and Antonia Sudkämper. "The who, when, and why of the glass cliff phenomenon: A meta-analysis of appointments to precarious leadership positions." *Psychological Bulletin* 146, no. 9 (2020): 797).

(Ryan, Michelle K., S. Alexander Haslam, Thekla Morgenroth, Floor Rink, Janka Stoker, and Kim Peters. "Getting on top of the glass cliff: Reviewing a decade of evidence, explanations, and impact." *Leadership Quarterly* 27, no. 3 (2016): 446–455).

Intersectionality Theory: An ideology advanced by Kimberlé Crenshaw (1989), intersectionality theory argues that race, gender, and class intersect to create formidable systemic barriers for women of color across a variety of sectors. Intersectionality theory emphasizes the reality that interlocking systems create barriers that seek to delegitimize the voices, experiences, and ideologies of Black women in particular (Apugo, 2019; Sanchez & Frey, 2020; Sales et al., Smith, 2022).

Piety: Dutifulness in religion (https://www.merriam-webster.com/dictionary/piety).

Sacred: Dedicated or set apart for the service or worship of a deity (https://www.merriam-webster.com/dictionary/sacred).

Secular: Of or relating to the worldly or temporal (https://www.merriam-webster.com/dictionary/secular).

White nationalism: One of a group of militant white people who espouse white supremacy (see white supremacy sense 1) and advocate enforced racial segregation (https://www.merriam-webster.com/dictionary/white%20nationalism).

Bibliography

Adeniyi-Ogunyankin, Grace, Moya Bailey, Karen Flynn, Bettina Judd, Anana Weekley, Jennifer Musial, and Melissa White. "Black Feminist Thought and the Gender, Women's, and Feminist Studies PhD: A Roundtable Discussion." *Feminist Formations*, 32 no.2, 1–28, https://doi.org/10.1353/ff.2020.0023.

Ahonen, Emily Q., Kaori Fujishiro, Thomas Cunningham, and Michael Flinn. "Work as an inclusive part of population health inequities research and prevention," *American Journal of Public Health*. 108 no.3 (2018): 306–11, https://doi.org/10.2105/AJPH.2017.304214.

Alexander, Michelle. 2010. *The New Jim Crow: Mass Incarceration in the Age of Colorblindness*. Chicago: Samuel Dewitt Proctor Conference, Inc.

Anderson, Amanda. "The Great Evil: Christianity, the Bible and the Native American Genocide," September 2, 2022, *Pioneer PBS*, https://www.pioneer.org/blogs/compass-stories/the-great-evil-christianity-the-bible-and-the-native-american-genocide/.

Apugo, Danielle. 2019. "A Hidden Culture of Coping: Insights on African American Women's Existence in Predominately White Institutions," *Multicultural Perspectives* 21 (1): 53–62, doi:10.1080/15210960.2019.1573067.

Barram, Michael Drew, Gimbiya Kettering, and Michael J. Rhodes. 2023. *Reparations and the Theological Disciplines*. Rowman & Littlefield.

Beckwith, LaShonda A., Danon R. Carter, and Tara Peters. "The Underrepresentation of African American Women in Executive Leadership: What's Getting in the Way?" *Journal of Business Studies Quarterly*, 7, no. 4 (2016): 115–134.

Boykin, Keith. *Why Does Everything Have to Be About Race?* (New York: Bold Type Books, 2024).

Bradley, L. Richard. "The Curse of Canaan and the American Negro," *Concordia Theological Monthly*, February 1, 1971, 42, No. 1, 10, https://scholar.csl.edu/ctm/vol42/iss1/10/.

Cheeks, Maura. "How Black Women Describe Navigating Race and Gender in the Workplace," *Harvard Business Review*, March 26, 2018, https://hbr.org/2018/03/how-black-women-describe-navigating-race-and-gender-in-the-workplace.

Craig, Robert. "Christianity and Empire: A Case Study of American Protestant Colonialism and Native Americans," *American Indian Culture and Research Journal*, 21, No.2, 1–41, https://escholarship.org/uc/item/5f29z35v.

Crenshaw, Kimberlé. "Demarginalizing the Intersection of Race and Sex: A Black Feminist Critique of Antidiscrimination Doctrine, Feminist Theory and Antiracist Politics," *University of Chicago Legal Forum*, 1 no. 8 (1989): 139–67.

Dawson, Rosie. "The 'white Christian problem': the doctrine of discovery that encouraged enslavement and lynchings," *Religion Media Centre*, September 11, 2023, https://religionmediacentre.org.uk/news/the-white-christian-problem-the-doctrine-of-discovery-that-encouraged-enslavement-and-lynchings/.

DiAngelo, Robin. *White Fragility: Why It's So Hard for White People to Talk About Racism*. (Boston: Beacon Press, 2020).

Dickens, Danielle D., Veronica Y. Womack, Treshae Dimes. "Managing Hypervisibility: An Exploration of Theory and Research on Identity Shifting Strategies in the Workplace Among Black Women." *Journal of Vocational*

Behavior 113, 153–163, https://doi.org/10.1016/j.jvb.2018.10.008.

DuMez, Kristin Kobes. *Jesus and John Wayne: How White Evangelicals Corrupted a Faith and Fractured a Nation* (New York: Liveright, 2020).

Frazier, E. Franklin. *Black Bourgeoisie: The Rise of a New Middle Class in the United States* (Englewood, NJ: Free Press, 1957).

Gamble, Erica D. and Norma J. Turner. "Career ascension of African American women in executive positions in postsecondary institutions," *Journal of Organizational Culture, Communications and Conflict* 19, no. 1 (2015).

Gomez-Bravo, Ana M. "The origins of Raza: Racializing Difference in Early Spanish," *Interfaces*, 2020, 7 No. 05, 64–114, DOI: 10.13130/interfaces-07-05.

Gonçalves dos Reis, João Carlos, and Sofia Menezes. "Gender Inequalities in the Military Service: A Systematic Literature Review," *Sexuality & Culture*, June 2020, DOI:10.1007/s12119-019-09662-y.

Hurston, Zora Neale. *Their Eyes Were Watching God* (Philadelphia: J.B. Lippincott, 1937).

Jeong, Seung-Hwan, Ann Mooney Murphy, and Yangyang Zhang. "Investor Reactions to Minority CEO Appointments: The Intersection of Race-Ethnicity and Gender," *Academy of Management*, July 26, 2021, https://journals.aom.org/doi/10.5465/AMBPP.2021.266.

Keith, Verna, and Cedric Herring. "Skin Tone and Stratification in the Black Community," *American Journal of Sociology*, 97 no. 3 (1991): 760–788, http://www.jstor.org/stable/2781783.

Kendi, Ibram X. *How to Be an Antiracist* (New York: One World, 2019).

Lorde, Audre. "The Master's Tools Will Never Dismantle the Master's House," *Sister Outsider: Essays and Speeches*, 1984, Ed. Berkeley: Crossing Press, 110–114, https://pressbooks.claremont.edu/clas112pomonavalentine/

chapter/lorde-audre-the-masters-tools-will-never-dismantle-the-masters-house/.

McCluney, Courtney L., Lauren L. Schmitz, Margaret T. Hicken, and Amanda Sonnega. "Structural racism in the workplace: Does perception matter for health inequalities?" *Social Science & Medicine*, February 2018, 199, 106–114, https://doi.org/10.1016/j.socscimed.2017.05.039.

McDowell, Jacqueline, and Akilah Carter-Francique. "An Intersectional Analysis of the Workplace Experiences of African American Female Athletic Directors," *Sex Roles*, 77 no. 5, (2017): 393–408, https://doi.org/10.1007/S11199-016-0730-Y.

McNeil, Brenda Salter. *Roadmap to Reconciliation: Moving Communities into Unity, Wholeness, and Justice* (Downers Grove, IL: InterVarsity Press, 2015).

Merrit, Keri Leigh. *Keeping Poor Whites and Blacks Apart: A Southern Tradition. The Bitter Southerner* Blog, 2023, https://bittersoutherner.com/from-the-southern-perspective/miscellany/what-you-dont-know-about-the-south.

Merrit, Keri Leigh. *Masterless men: poor whites and slavery in the Antebellum South* (Cambridge: Cambridge University Press, 2017), https://doi.org/10.1017/9781316875568.

Morgenroth, Thekla, Teri A. Kirby, Michelle K. Ryan, and Antonia Sudkämper. 2020. "The Who, When, and Why of the Glass Cliff Phenomenon: A Meta-Analysis of Appointments to Precarious Leadership Positions." *Psychological Bulletin*, 146.

Morrison, Toni. *The Bluest Eye* (New York: Vintage Books, 1970).

National Archives, "Declaration of Independence: A Transcription," *The Declaration of Independence*, n.d., https://www.archives.gov/founding-docs/declaration-transcript.

Nelson, Anne. *Shadow Network: Media, Money, and the Secret Hub of the Radical Right* (New York: Bloomsbury Publishing, 2019).

Pappas, Stephanie. "Effective therapy with Black women," *Monitor on Psychology* 52 no.8 (2021): 38, http://www.apa.org/monitor/2021/11/ce-therapy-black-women.

Platt Lisa F., and Sandy C. Fanning. "The strong Black woman concept: Associated demographic characteristics and perceived stress among Black women," *Journal of Black Psychology,* 49 No. 1, (2022): 58-84, https://doi.org/10.1177/00957984221096211.

Porter, Anthony Peyton. "Jump at de sun: The Story of Zora Neale Hurston," Carolrhoda Books, 1992, https://www.adl.org/jump-de-sun-story-zora-neale-hurston.

Potok, Mark, and Laurie Wood. "Leaving White Nationalism," *Southern Poverty Law Center,* August 2013, Fall Issue, https://www.splcenter.org/fighting-hate/intelligence-report/2013/leaving-white-nationalism.

Robinson, Lori, and Michael E. O'Hanlon. "Women Warriors: The Ongoing Story of Integrating and Diversifying the Armed Forces," *Brookings Institution,* 2020, https://www.brookings.edu/articles/women-warriors-the-ongoing-story-of-integrating-and-diversifying-the-armed-forces/.

Ryan, Michelle K, S. Alexander Haslam, Thekla Morgenroth, Rink Floor, Janka Stoker, and Kim Peter. "Getting on top of the glass cliff: Reviewing a decade of evidence, explanations, and impact," *Leadership Quarterly* 27, no. 3 (2016): 446–55.

Schaller, Tom, and Paul Waldman. *White Rural Rage: The Threat to American Democracy* (New York: Penguin Random House, 2024).

Smith, Christine A. *Beyond the Stained Glass Ceiling: Equipping and Encouraging Female Pastors* (Valley Forge, PA: Judson Press, 2013).

Smith, Christine A. "Lived Experiences of Inequity of African American Women Leading Struggling, Nonprofit Organizations in the United States: A Phenomenological

Study," Dissertation, Capella University, 2022, *ProQuest Dissertations Publishing*, 28964693.

Tobin-Tyler, Elizabeth. "Intimate partner violence, firearm injuries and homicides: A health justice approach to two intersecting public health crises," *Journal of Law, Medicine, and Ethics*, May 25, 2023, 5 No 1, 64–76, doi: 10.1017/jme.2023.41. PMID: 37226755; PMCID: PMC10209983.

Ujlaki, Stephen, Co-Director, Christopher Jones. *Bad Faith: Christian Nationalism's Unholy War on Democracy*, San Francisco: The Film Sales Company, 2024.

Watson, Thomas E. "The Negro Question in the South," *The Arena,* VI (October 1892): 540–550, https://msuweb.montclair.edu/~furrg/spl/tomwatson.html.

Zakaria, Fareed. *Age of Revolutions: Progress and Backlash from 1600 to the Present* (Random House, 2024).